SPIRITUAL GIFTS ENCOUNTER

PART ONE OF THE DEVELOPING GIFTS AND SKILLS SERIES

DR. HENDRIK J VORSTER

CONTENTS

Spiritual Gifts Encounter   v

Part I   1

1. Introduction   3
2. The Ministerial Office Gifts   14
3. The Service Gifts   36
4. The Supernatural Spiritual Gifts   57
5. Discovering Your Spiritual Gifts   82
6. Vorster Spiritual Gifts Questionnaire   85
7. Vorster Gifts Score Sheet   96

PART II

1. Other Books by Dr Hendrik J Vorster   105

Endnotes   115

SPIRITUAL GIFTS ENCOUNTER
PART ONE OF THE DEVELOPING GIFTS AND SKILLS SERIES

-- Disciple Manual --

Spiritual Gifts Encounter
Part One of the Developing Gifts and Skills Series
Disciple Manual
By Dr. Hendrik J. Vorster

Copyright © 2021 by Hendrik J. Vorster.

All rights reserved. No part of this book may be used or reproduced by any means, graphic, electronic, or mechanical, including photocopying, recording, taping or by any information storage retrieval system without the written permission of the author except in the case of brief quotations embodied in critical articles and reviews.

This book is a work of non-fiction. Unless otherwise noted, the author and the publisher make no explicit guarantees as to the accuracy of the information contained in this book and in some cases, names of people and places have been altered to protect their privacy.

For more copies and information please visit and write to us at: www.churchplantinginstitute.com
resources@churchplantinginstitute.com

Because of the dynamic nature of the Internet, any web addresses or links contained in this book may have changed since publication and may no longer be valid. The views expressed in this work are solely those of the author and do not necessarily reflect the views of the publisher, and the publisher hereby disclaims any responsibility for them.

Scripture quotations marked AMP are taken from the Amplified Bible, Copyright 2015 by the Lockman Foundation. Used by permission.

Scripture quotations marked NIV are taken from e Holy Bible, New International Version, NIV Copyright 1973, 1978, 1984, 2011 by Biblica, Inc. Used by permission. All rights reserved worldwide.

Scripture quotations marked KJV are taken from the King James Version.

ISBN 13-978-1-955923-13-2

PART I

SPIRITUAL GIFTS ENCOUNTER

Part One of the Developing Gifts and Skills Series

1
INTRODUCTION
SESSION ONE

God saved us to _____!
God saved us to serve. To serve the purpose of God well, we need to be appropriately equipped.

God equips us with Spiritual _____ to serve!

The way God equips His people is by giving them Gifts and Abilities, and we call these Spiritual Gifts. Knowing and Understanding Spiritual Gifts and how God uses these in and through our lives, empowers us to minister more effectively to the Building up of the Body of Christ.

What Is a Spiritual Gift?

> *"A Spiritual Gift is a distinguishing _____ given to us, by the Holy Spirit, specifically to build the Body of Christ up for their _____."*

Spiritual Gifts

The Bible teaches that every believer is, and should function as, a vital part of the body of Christ. He has endowed the members with special abilities and ministries for the benefit of the body as a whole, both locally and worldwide.

_____ abilities are not Spiritual Giftedness

Let's first discuss talents, or natural abilities. A natural ability may be something you're born with, like physical co-ordination, or, it may be a talent you've developed through the years, such as playing a musical instrument.

These natural abilities or talents may be useful or entertaining, but they deal primarily with the surfaces of life.

Spiritual Gifts are therefore abilities graciously given to us by the Holy Spirit. The purpose for the activation of these Gifts in our lives are for the building up and edification of the Body of Christ.

The Nature of Spiritual Gifts

1. Spiritual Gifts are _____ abilities, powers and operations.

Spiritual Gifts are bestowed, by the Holy Spirit, for the use of Believers only.

> *1 Corinthians 12:7 (NIV)*
> *"Now to each one the manifestation of the Spirit is given for the common good."*

Spiritual gifts are not just human talents, they are Divinely Inspired abilities, powers and operations.

> *1 Corinthians 12:28 (NIV)* "And **God has placed in the church** first *of all apostles, second prophets, third teachers, then miracles,*

then gifts of healing, of helping, of guidance, and of different kinds of tongues."

The gifts of healings and tongues are right in the midst of the gifts of helps and administration. Even though some Gifts seem to be more explicitly prominent and visible than others, they operate by the same Holy Spirit, for the same purpose.

2. Spiritual Gifts are _____ for Believers.

Spiritual gifts are gifts given graciously to His people. The word for gifts is "charismata" which literally means "graciously given." This means that it is graciously given for our use. It is given for a purpose.

1 Peter 4:10 (NIV)
*Each of you should use whatever gift you have received to serve others, **as faithful stewards of God's grace** in its various forms.*

3. Spiritual gifts are to be _____, and not treated or treasured just like ordinary trophies.

We are all encouraged to serve and use our Gifts in the measure of faith we received. We should be humbled by the fact that we have been blessed to possess Spiritual Gifts.

1 Peter 4:10 (NIV)
***Each of you should use whatever gift you have received to serve others,** as faithful stewards of God's grace in its various forms.*

4. Spiritual gifts operate by _____ and must be _____ and nurtured.

Spiritual Gifts are received by impartation, through the laying on of Hands.

1 Timothy 4:14 (NIV)
*Do not neglect your gift, **which was given you through prophecy when the body of elders laid their hands on you.***

2 Timothy 1:6 (NIV)
"For this reason I remind you to fan into flame the gift of God, which is in you through the laying on of my hands."

Spiritual Gifts are exercised according to one's faith.

Romans 12:6 (NIV)
*"We have different gifts, according to the grace given to each of us. If your gift is prophesying, then **prophesy in accordance with your faith**; if it is serving, then serve; if it is teaching, then teach; if it is to encourage, then give encouragement; if it is giving, then give generously; if it is to lead, do it diligently; if it is to show mercy, do it cheerfully."*

Spiritual Gifts are subject to the will of the user.

1 Corinthians 14:32 (NIV)
"The spirits of prophets are subject to the control of prophets."

The Bible teaches that Spiritual Gifts should be encouraged and nurtured.

1 Corinthians 14:1 (NIV)
*Follow the way of love **and eagerly desire gifts of the Spirit**, especially prophecy.*

1 Corinthians 14:12 (NIV)
*"So it is with you. **Since you are eager for gifts of the Spirit, try to excel in those that build up the church.**"*

1 Corinthians 14:39 (NIV)
*Therefore, my brothers and sisters, **be eager to prophesy**, and do not forbid speaking in tongues.*

2 Timothy 1:6 (NIV)
*"For this reason I remind you to **fan into flame the gift of God**, which is in you through the laying on of my hands."*

We should be eager for Spiritual Gifts.

1 Corinthians 12:31 (NIV)
*"31 Now **eagerly desire the greater gifts**. Love Is Indispensable, And yet I will show you the most excellent way."*

1 Corinthians 14:1 (NIV)
"1 Follow the way of love and eagerly desire gifts of the Spirit, especially prophecy."

1 Corinthians 14:12 (NIV)
*12 So it is with you. **Since you are eager for gifts of the Spirit, try to excel** in those that build up the church.*

5. Spiritual Gifts are given for the _____ of the Body of Christ.

The true purpose of Spiritual Gifts are for edification.

1 Corinthians 12:7 (NIV)
*"Now to each one the manifestation of **the Spirit is given for the common good.**"*

1 Corinthians 14:4 (NIV)
*Anyone who speaks in a tongue edifies themselves, **but the one who prophesies edifies the church.***

1 Corinthians 14:26 (NIV)
*What then shall we say, brothers and sisters? When you come together, each of you has a hymn, or a word of instruction, a revelation, a tongue or an interpretation. **Everything must be done so that the church may be built up.***

Spiritual Gifts are to bring glory to the Lord Jesus.

1 Peter 4:10,11 (NIV)
*"Each of you should use whatever gift you have received to serve others, as faithful stewards of God's grace in its various forms. If anyone speaks, they should do so as one who speaks the very words of God. If anyone serves, they should do so with the strength God provides, **so that in all things God may be praised through Jesus Christ.** To him be the glory and the power for ever and ever. Amen"*

What you will find in the next few pages should not be used merely as an assessment, but as an exploration tool to allow the Holy Spirit to quicken His Grace and Gifts within your heart.

The following Scriptures explores the Spiritual Gifts of the Holy Spirit. These Scriptures exhorts us to pursue them and be eager for their assimilation and use in our lives.

1 Corinthians 12:1 (NIV) Spiritual Gifts
"[12:1] Now about spiritual gifts, brothers, I do not want you to be ignorant."

1 Corinthians 14:1 (NIV) Gifts of Prophecy and Tongues "[14:1] Follow the way of love and eagerly desire spiritual gifts, especially the gift of prophecy."

1 Corinthians 14:12 (NIV)
"[12] So it is with you. Since you are eager to have spiritual gifts, try to excel in gifts that build up the church."

1 Corinthians 14:39-40 (NIV)
"Therefore, my brothers, be eager to prophesy, and do not forbid speaking in tongues. [40] But everything should be done in a fitting and orderly way."

Historical re-emergence of the Holy Spirit.

Before we head into looking at the **three Parts of the Spiritual Gifts**, let us look at the contemporary historical re-emergence of the Holy Spirit.

One of the distinctives of the Church in Acts, and the New Testament Churches that was planted, is their emphasis on the supernatural gifts of the Spirit at work in the church. Throughout the evolving church history there remained a remnant who always embraced an openness to the work and ministry of the Holy Spirit.

During the latter half of the nineteenth century, many people from across the denominational spectrum experienced and embraced these workings of the Holy Spirit and the Gracious Gifts He blessed them with. The Pentecostal and Charismatic Churches evolved as the prominence of the Holy Spirit's work gained renewed acceptance.

The acceptance of the Person and work of the Holy Spirit has never been confined to these denominations only, but as we observe, His work is seen and appreciated by most Believers around the world, regardless of denominational affiliation. Unfortunately, there's been some diverse theories and practices, including some misuse and abuse, which accompanied this renewal of spiritual gifts. Regardless, the Holy Spirit is here with us, as Jesus promised, and He is surely working marvellously to build the Church through His people.

While experience must not be our authority, it serves a vital role in developing a practical understanding of this subject.

At the beginning of the twentieth century, the early Pentecostals discovered the biblical teaching about the baptism of the Holy Spirit, speaking in tongues, and the gifts of the Spirit, and they in earnest sought to receive and implement these truths. As God poured out His

Spirit with signs following, what they once found obscure, mysterious, or merely theoretical, suddenly became a clear and living reality. As they followed the leading of the Spirit, they corrected misconceptions and abuses by referring back to the Bible and its explanation of the purpose and operation of spiritual gifts.

Spiritual Gifts are defined and explained in three parts:

There is primarily three main portions of Scripture that describe and define Spiritual Gifts. These portions helps us see them in their specific assignment for our lives. Let us take a brief overview of these three differentiations.

Three passages in the New Testament—Romans 12, Ephesians 4, and I Corinthians 12—list some gifts that God has granted the church.

1. Romans 12 discusses abilities, talents, or functions that God gives to all believers. These are commonly known as **Service Gifts.**
2. Ephesians 4 identifies special offices of leadership and ministry that God has given to the church. These are known as **Ministerial office gifts.**
3. In I Corinthians 12 and 14 we find supernatural signs, wonders, and miracles that occur by the direct empowerment and operation of the Holy Spirit through His people. These are known as **Supernatural Spiritual Gifts.**

For the sake of clarity, we will label these three lists respectively as the service gifts, the ministerial office gifts, and the supernatural gifts.

OFFICE GIFTS (Ephesians 4:11)

The Ministerial Gifts are primarily found in Ephesians chapter 4 and is commonly known as the Five-fold Ministry Gifts.

Ephesians 4:11-12 (NIV)
*[11] It was he who gave some to be **apostles**, some to be **prophets**, some to be **evangelists**, and some to be **pastors** and **teachers**, [12] to prepare God's people for works of service, so that the body of Christ may be built up.*

- Apostle
- Prophet
- Evangelist
- Pastor
- Teacher

GIFTS (Romans 12:3-8)

The Service Gifts are recorded primarily in Romans chapter 12 and is frequently referred to as the Service Gifts.

Romans 12:3-8 (NIV)
*"For I say, through **the grace given to me**, to **everyone** who is among you, not to think of himself more highly than he ought to think, but to think soberly, as God has dealt to each one a measure of faith. For as we have many members in one body, but all the members do not have the same function, so we, being many, are one body in Christ, and individually members of one another. Having then gifts differing according to the grace that is given to us, let us use them: if **prophecy**, let us prophesy in proportion to our faith; or **ministry**, let us use it in our ministering; he who **teaches**, in teaching; he who **exhorts**, in exhortation; he who **gives**, with liberality; he who **leads**, with diligence; he who shows **mercy**, with cheerfulness"*

- Prophecy
- Ministry (Serving)
- Teaching
- Exhortation

- Giving
- Leading (ruling in KJV)
- Showing mercy

SUPERNATURAL _____ GIFTS (1 Corinthians 12:1-9)

The Supernatural Spiritual Gifts are specifically explored in the First Book to the Church in Corinth. The extensive use of these gifts is seen throughout the New Testament writings.

> *1 Corinthians 12:7-11 (NIV)*
> *[7] Now to each one the manifestation of the Spirit is given for the common good. [8] To one there is given through the Spirit the message of **wisdom**, to another the message of **knowledge** by means of the same Spirit, [9] to another **faith** by the same Spirit, to another **gifts of healing** by that one Spirit, [10] to another **miraculous powers**, to another **prophecy**, to another **distinguishing between spirits**, to another speaking in different kinds of **tongues**,* and to still another the **interpretation of tongues**.* [11] All these are the work of one and the same Spirit, and he gives them to each one, just as he determines.*

- Word of wisdom
- Word of knowledge
- Faith
- Gifts of healings
- Working of miracles
- Prophecy (Explored under Service Gifts)
- Discerning of spirits
- Different kinds of tongues
- Interpretation of tongues

In the following sessions we will look at each of these general groupings in a more detailed manner.

Assimilation Sheet for Introduction to Spiritual Gifts

1. Complete the sentence. *God saved us to _____!*
2. What is a Spiritual Gift?
   _____
   _____

3. Complete the sentence. *Spiritual Gifts are _____ abilities, powers and operations.*
4. Complete the sentence. *Spiritual Gifts are _____ for Believers.*
5. Complete the sentence. *Spiritual Gifts are to be _____ and not treated or treasured just like ordinary trophies.*
6. Complete the sentence. *Spiritual Gifts operate by _____ and must be _____ and nurtured.*
7. Complete the sentence. *Spiritual Gifts are given for the _____ of the Body of Christ.*
8. Name the three parts of the Spiritual Gifts. Give at least one Scriptural reference to substantiate.
   1. _____
   2. _____
   3. _____
9. Name the Ministerial Office Gifts.
   1. _____
   2. _____
   3. _____
   4. _____
   5. _____
10. Name two Service Gifts.
    1. _____
    2. _____
11. Name two Supernatural Spiritual Gifts.
    1. _____
    2. _____

2

THE MINISTERIAL OFFICE GIFTS
SESSION TWO

During this session we will be exploring the Ministerial Gifts.

Ephesians 4:11-12 (NIV)
*[11] It was he who gave some to be **apostles**, some to be **prophets**, some to be **evangelists**, and some to be **pastors** and **teachers**, [12] to prepare God's people for works of service, so that the body of Christ may be built up.*

Ephesians 4:8 (KJV) Therefore He says: 'When He ascended on high, He led captivity captive, and gave gifts to men.'

*Ephesians 4:11-16 (KJV) And He Himself gave some to be **apostles**, some **prophets**, some **evangelists**, and some **pastors** and **teachers**, for the equipping of the saints for the work of ministry, for the edifying of the body of Christ, till we all come to the unity of the faith and the knowledge of the Son of God, to a perfect man, to the measure of the stature of the fullness of Christ; that we should no longer be children, tossed to and fro and carried about with every wind of doctrine, by the trickery*

> *of men, in the cunning craftiness by which they lie in wait to deceive, but, speaking the truth in love, may grow up in all things into Him who is the head—Christ— from whom the whole body, joined and knit together by what every joint supplies, according to the effective working by which every part does its share, causes growth of the body for the edifying of itself in love"*

This passage introduces to us what is often called the **fivefold ministry**. The five ministries listed are not simply God's gifts to individuals within the church, but they are God's gifts (Greek, *dogmata*) to the church as a whole. While Romans 12 speaks of abilities or functions, using both nouns and verbs to describe the operation of the service gifts, Ephesians 4 speaks of offices, using nouns to designate them. The indication is that the gifts of Ephesians 4 are more formal or defined ministries in and for the whole church. When Jesus ascended to Heaven, He gave gifts to the church— the ministers of the gospel.

As the passage reveals, the people who hold these offices are recognized leaders in the church, **responsible for equipping** others and thereby helping the church **to function effectively, grow into maturity,** and **become established in doctrinal truth.** The nature of their work requires that they be preachers of the gospel. In modern terminology, we typically call them '**Pastor**' or '**Priest**,' using this designation in a special sense, even though in the KJV and NKJV the term *minister* is a general one signifying a servant or worker.

Let us now take a few moments to look at each of these Ministerial Office Gifts:

1. Apostle.

An **apostle** (Greek, *Apostolos*) is literally someone sent on a mission, a messenger, an ambassador, or as a commissioner. Although no one can take the place of the twelve apostles of the Lamb (Revelation 21:14), who were eyewitnesses of Christ, others fulfill an apostolic office by serving as pioneer missionaries and leaders of other ministers.

Revelation 21:14 (NIV)
*The wall of the city had twelve foundations, and on them were the names of **the twelve apostles of the Lamb**.*

During the Lord Jesus' earthly ministry, after first calling some to follow Him and to be His Disciples, He one day, after a night in prayer, appointed some of His Disciples to become the first Apostles, His Sent ones.

Luke 6:12-13 (NIV) The Twelve Apostles
*"12 One of those days **Jesus went out to a mountainside to pray**, and spent the night praying to God. 13 **When morning came, he called his disciples to him and chose twelve of them, whom he also designated apostles.**"*

Mark 3:13-19 (NIV) The Appointing of the Twelve Apostles
*13 Jesus went up on a mountainside and **called to him those he wanted, and they came to him. 14 He appointed twelve— designating them apostles—that they might be with him and that he might send them out to preach 15 and to have authority to drive out demons.** 16 These are the twelve he appointed: Simon (to whom he gave the name Peter); 17 James son of Zebedee and his brother John (to them he gave the name Boanerges, which means Sons of Thunder); 18 Andrew, Philip, Bartholomew, Matthew, Thomas, James son of Alphaeus, Thaddaeus, Simon the Zealot 19 and Judas Iscariot, who betrayed him.*

Matthew 10:7-8 (NIV)
As you go, preach this message: 'The kingdom of heaven is near.' 8 Heal the sick, raise the dead, cleanse those who have leprosy, drive out demons. Freely you have received, freely give.

From these two accounts we learn that Jesus chose twelve from among all His Disciples and appointed them as Apostles.

The reference in the Gospel of Mark helps us understand the special designation, as Apostles. The Bible says: *"that they might be with him and that he might send them out to preach 15 and to have authority to drive out demons."*

The designation – Apostle – indicates that they were **appointed with an entrustment**, like John the Baptist, to go ahead of the Lord Jesus to preach wherever He might send them, with His blessing and designated authority, and empowerment to *"heal the sick, raise the dead, and to drive out demons."*

Apostleship was not only confined to the twelve Apostles.

One of the amazing blessings the New Testament Church received was the continuation of the Lord to appoint Apostles, as Gifts to the Church.

Apostles Paul and Barnabas

In the church at Antioch, whilst fasting and praying, the Holy Spirit spoke and instructed that Paul and Barnabas be sent out for the work they were called for. After prayer and the laying on of hands, they sent Paul and Barnabas as pioneer missionaries, and they became known as apostles even though neither were part of the original Twelve.

> *Acts 13:2 (NIV)*
> *"While they were worshiping the Lord and fasting, the Holy Spirit said, "Set apart for me **Barnabas and Saul** for the work to which I have called them." 3 So after they had fasted and prayed, they placed their hands on them and sent them off. 4 The two of them, sent on their way by the Holy Spirit, went down to Seleucia and sailed from there to Cyprus"*

Later in the Book of Acts we read about *"the Apostles Barnabas and Paul."*

> *Acts 14:14 (NIV)*
> *But when **the apostles Barnabas and Paul** heard of this, they tore their clothes and rushed out into the crowd, shouting:*

On a few occasions we see how Paul defends His Apostleship.

> *1 Corinthians 9:2 (NIV)*
> *Even though I may not be an apostle to others, surely, I am to you!* ***For you are the seal of my apostleship in the Lord.***

The Apostle Paul open his pastoral letters with the words "Paul, an Apostle" often.

> *Galatians 1:1 (NIV)*
> ***"Paul, an apostle**—sent not from men nor by man, but by Jesus Christ and God the Father, who raised him from the dead—"*

In the Pastoral Letter to the church in Galatia Paul trumps the case for his Apostleship as an Apostle to the Gentiles just as Peter was an Apostle to the Jews.

> *Galatians 2:8-9 (NIV)*
> *"For God, who was at work in the ministry of **Peter as an apostle to the Jews**, was also at work in my ministry as **an apostle to the Gentiles.** 9 James, Peter and John, those reputed to be pillars, **gave me and Barnabas the right hand of fellowship** when they recognized the grace given to me. They agreed that we should go to the Gentiles, and they to the Jews."*

In the Pastoral Letter to the church in Corinth he defends the ministry of an Apostle.

1 Corinthians 4:1 (NIV) **Apostles of Christ**
So then, men ought to regard us as servants of Christ and as those entrusted with the secret things of God.

1 Corinthians 4:9 (NIV)
*For it seems to me that **God has put us apostles** on display at the end of the procession, like men condemned to die in the arena. We have been made a spectacle to the whole universe, to angels as well as to men.*

1 Corinthians 9:1-2 (NIV) **The Rights of an Apostle**
Am I not free? Am I not an apostle? Have I not seen Jesus our Lord? Are you not the result of my work in the Lord? 2 Even though I may not be an apostle to others, surely, I am to you! For you are the seal of my apostleship in the Lord.

The signs of an Apostle is clearly outlined in the second Book of Corinthians.

2 Corinthians 12:12 (NIV)
[12] The things that mark an apostle—signs, wonders and miracles — were done among you with great perseverance.

Likewise, James the Lord's brother, not one of the original twelve, was called an apostle.

Galatians 1:19 (NIV)
*I saw none of **the other apostles–only James, the Lord's brother**. Although he was not one of the Twelve, he was the leader of the church in Jerusalem.*

Acts 15:13 (NIV)
*When they finished, **James** spoke up: "Brothers, listen to me. "*

The term Apostle/s is found 22/71 times respectively in the NIV translation. It is translated **apostle most times;** *messenger or worker* on a couple of times (2 Corinthians. 8: 23; Phil 2: 25); and **once more as a messenger in John** (John. 13: 16).

> *2 Corinthians 8:23 (NIV)*
> *As for Titus, he is my partner and **fellow worker** among you; as for our brothers, they are representatives of the churches and an honor to Christ.*

> *Philippians 2:25 (NIV)*
> *But I think it is necessary to send back to you Epaphroditus, my brother, **fellow worker** and fellow soldier, who is also your **messenger**, whom you sent to take care of my needs.*

> *John 13:16 (NIV)*
> *I tell you the truth, no servant is greater than his master, nor is a **messenger** greater than the one who sent him.*

At least twenty-four Apostles are recorded in the New Testament:

- Simon Peter and his brother Andrew (Mt. 10: 2)
- James, son of Zebedee and John his brother (Mt. 10: 2)
- Philip and his brother Bartholomew (Mt. 10: 3)
- James, son of Alphaeus and Judas his brother (Luke 6: 16) and
- Matthew, son of Alphaeus, perhaps brother of James and Judas (Mk. 2: 14; Lk. 6: 15)
- Thomas (Mt. 10: 3)
- Simon Zelotes, brother of James and Judas, according to tradition (Lk. 6: 15)
- Judas Iscariot (Mt. 10: 4)
- Matthias (Acts 1: 26)
- Barnabas (1Cor. 9: 5-6 Acts 13: 1-3; 14: 4, 14; Gal. 2: 9)
- Andronicus (Rom. 16: 7)

- Junia (Rom. 16: 7)
- Apollos (1Cor. 4: 6- 9)
- James, the Lord's brother (Gal. 1: 19; 2: 6; Jas. 1: 1)
- Silas (1Th. 1: 1; 2: 6)
- Timothy (1Th. 1: 1; 2: 6)
- Titus (2Cor. 8: 23)
- Epaphroditus (Php. 2: 25)
- Paul (Gal. 1: 1; 2: 8)
- Jesus Christ (Heb. 3: 1)

The Apostle Paul says in Ephesians chapter 4 that the Lord gave gifts to the church, and these equipping gifts are: Apostles, Prophets, Evangelists, Pastors and Teachers.

Ephesians 4:11-13 (NIV)
*"[11] It was **he who gave some to be apostles**, some to be prophets, some to be evangelists, and some to be pastors and teachers, [12] to prepare God's people for works of service, so that the body of Christ may be built up [13] until we all reach unity in the faith and in the knowledge of the Son of God and become mature, attaining to the whole measure of the fullness of Christ."*

In conclusion of learning about the existence of Apostles, and what defines them and their work, let us answer a few discovery questions.

Discovery Questions.

The answers to the following few questions might be telltale signs that might help you to affirm your designation as an Apostle.

- Do you have a strong sense that God anointed you to be a leader, and do you find yourself often taking the lead among Believers?
- Do you have the confident faith that wherever God might

be sending you, that you will be able to lead people to Christ and Disciple them into maturity?
- Do you find that people often follow your instructions?
- Do you naturally dream and envision new churches planted?
- Do people often ask you to serve in leadership positions because of your ability to make things happen?
- Do you have a strong sense of God's Call on your life to pioneer new ministries?
- Have you been able to successfully pioneer new churches before?

If the answer to all of these statements is a strong *"YES"* then you most certainly have been anointed by God as an Apostolic Leader to advance His Church. If the answer is more *"YES, sometimes"* then you should certainly open yourself up to the possibility that the Lord desire to increasingly use you to pioneer new ministries for Him. If the answer is a *"NO, I have never sensed such an urge or prompting,"* then you might be one of those precious believers who has been blessed with some other prominent gift to serve the Body of Christ.

2. Prophet.

A **prophet** is one who imparts and delivers special, divinely inspired, messages and directions from God.

> *Acts 11:27-30 (NIV)*
> *27 During this time some prophets came down from Jerusalem to Antioch. 28 One of them, named **Agabus**, **stood up and through the Spirit predicted that a severe famine would spread over the entire Roman world**. (This happened during the reign of Claudius.) 29 The disciples, as each one was able, decided to provide help for the brothers and sisters living in Judea. 30 This they did, sending their gift to the elders by Barnabas and Saul.*

Acts 15:32 (NIV)
***32 Judas and Silas, who themselves were prophets,** said much to encourage and strengthen the believers.*

Acts 21:10-14 (NIV)
*10 After we had been there a number of days, **a prophet named Agabus** came down from Judea. 11 Coming over to us, he took Paul's belt, tied his own hands and feet with it and said, **"The Holy Spirit says, 'In this way the Jewish leaders in Jerusalem will bind the owner of this belt and will hand him over to the Gentiles.'"***
*12 When we heard this, we and the people there pleaded with Paul not to go up to Jerusalem. 13 Then Paul answered, "Why are you weeping and breaking my heart? I am ready not only to be bound, but also to die in Jerusalem for the name of the Lord Jesus." 14 When he would not be dissuaded, we gave up and said, **"The Lord's will be done."***

While many people in the church may prophesy from time to time, the office of a prophet is filled by someone whom God consistently uses in this manner in his public ministry. All preachers should preach the Word of God and preach under the anointing of the Holy Spirit, but the prophet is specially called and enabled to proclaim the specific will, purpose, and counsel of God to His people. He will frequently communicate messages concerning God's plan for the future or the church's need to take action in God's plan.

Prophets are those who speak for God.

Hebrews 1: 1 (NIV)
"1 In the past God spoke to our ancestors through the prophets at many times and in various ways,"

Acts 3: 21 (NIV)
21 Heaven must receive him until the time comes for God to restore everything, as he promised long ago through his holy prophets.

Prophets are primarily preachers of righteousness, who bring messages of encouragement, strengthening and comfort.

> *Acts 15: 32-34 (NIV)*
> *32 Judas and Silas, who themselves were prophets, said much to encourage and strengthen the believers. 33 After spending some time there, they were sent off by the believers with the blessing of peace to return to those who had sent them. [34] 35 But Paul and Barnabas remained in Antioch, where they and many others taught and preached the word of the Lord.*

> *1Corinthians 14: 3-5 (NIV)*
> *3 But the one who prophesies speaks to people for their strengthening, encouraging and comfort. 4 Anyone who speaks in a tongue edifies themselves, but the one who prophesies edifies the church. 5 I would like every one of you to speak in tongues, but I would rather have you prophesy. The one who prophesies is greater than the one who speaks in tongues, unless someone interprets, so that the church may be edified.*

Sometimes Prophets foretell the future.

> *Luke 24: 44-49 (NIV)*
> *He said to them, "This is what I told you while I was still with you: Everything must be fulfilled that is written about me in the Law of Moses, the Prophets and the Psalms." Then he opened their minds so they could understand the Scriptures. 46 He told them, "This is what is written: The Messiah will suffer and rise from the dead on the third day, 47 and repentance for the forgiveness of sins will be preached in his name to all nations, beginning at Jerusalem. 48 You are witnesses of these things. 49 I am going to send you what my Father has promised; but stay in the city until you have been clothed with power from on high."*

Prophecy is one of the gifts of the Spirit.

1Corinthians 12:10 (NIV)
10 to another miraculous powers, to another prophecy, to another distinguishing between spirits, to another speaking in different kinds of tongues,"

The office of a Prophet is next in importance to apostles.

1 Corinthians 12:28-31 (NIV)
"28 And God has placed in the church first of all apostles, second prophets, third teachers, then miracles, then gifts of healing, of helping, of guidance, and of different kinds of tongues. 29 Are all apostles? Are all prophets? Are all teachers? Do all work miracles? 30 Do all have gifts of healing? Do all speak in tongues? Do all interpret? 31 Now eagerly desire the greater gifts."

Those who exercise this gift are known as prophets as well.

Acts 13:1-3 (NIV)
1 Now in the church at Antioch there were prophets and teachers: Barnabas, Simeon called Niger, Lucius of Cyrene, Manaen (who had been brought up with Herod the tetrarch) and Saul. 2 While they were worshiping the Lord and fasting, the Holy Spirit said, "Set apart for me Barnabas and Saul for the work to which I have called them." 3 So after they had fasted and prayed, they placed their hands on them and sent them off."

Directions for the exercise of this gift are found in 1Corinthians chapter 14.

1Samuel 19:18-24 (NIV)
18 When David had fled and made his escape, he went to Samuel at Ramah and told him all that Saul had done to him. Then he

and Samuel went to Naioth and stayed there. 19 Word came to Saul: "David is in Naioth at Ramah"; 20 so he sent men to capture him. But when they saw a group of prophets prophesying, with Samuel standing there as their leader, the Spirit of God came on Saul's men, and they also prophesied. 21 Saul was told about it, and he sent more men, and they prophesied too. Saul sent men a third time, and they also prophesied. 22 Finally, he himself left for Ramah and went to the great cistern at Seku. And he asked, "Where are Samuel and David?" "Over in Naioth at Ramah," they said. 23 So Saul went to Naioth at Ramah. But the Spirit of God came even on him, and he walked along prophesying until he came to Naioth. 24 He stripped off his garments, and he too prophesied in Samuel's presence. He lay naked all that day and all that night. This is why people say, "Is Saul also among the prophets?"

2 Chronicles 9: 29 (NIV)
*29 As for the other events of Solomon's reign, from beginning to end, are they not written in the records of **Nathan the prophet**, in **the prophecy of Ahijah** the Shilonite and in **the visions of Iddo the seer** concerning Jeroboam son of Nebat?*

In conclusion of learning about Prophets, and what defines them and their work, let us answer a few discovery questions.

Discovery Questions.

The answers to the following few questions might be telltale signs that God might have anointed you as a Prophet.

- Do you have a strong experience of seeing things, which God shows you, before they happen?
- Do you frequently see that the direct and special messages God gives you impact people greatly?

- Have you experienced that people were deeply offended when you brought them the message God gave you?
- Do you frequently find yourself praying for messages of God to deliver to His people?
- Do you often get asked to pray to God for direction about people's life situations?
- Do you have a strong sense and confidence that God reveals and speaks through you to others?
- Do you often find yourself seeing people's lives as open books before you?
- Do you often hear how things happened just as God said it would through messages you delivered to people?
- Do you find yourself naturally tuned in to hear what God is saying, or want to say, through you to people?

If the answer to all of these statements is a strong *"YES"* then you most certainly have been anointed by God as a Prophet to the Church. If the answer is more *"YES, sometimes"* then you should certainly open yourself up to the possibility that the Lord desire to increasingly use you to hear, receive and deliver His direct, personal messages to people. If the answer is a *"NO, I have never sensed such an urge or prompting,"* then you might be one of those precious believers who has been blessed with some other prominent gift to serve the Body of Christ.

3. Evangelist.

An **evangelist** is literally a preacher of the gospel. He proclaims the good news for the benefit of the unsaved. Greek – **euangelistes**, literally means **the bringer of glad tidings.**

> *Acts 21:8-9 (NIV)*
> *[8] Leaving the next day, we reached Caesarea and stayed at the house of **Philip the evangelist**, one of the Seven. [9] He had four unmarried daughters who prophesied.*

2 Timothy 4:5 (NIV)

*[5] But you, keep your head in all situations, endure hardship, do **the work of an evangelist**, discharge all the duties of your ministry.*

This biblical term is not limited to the modern usage of an itinerant preacher who holds special services. Rather, it connotes a minister who is **particularly effective in winning souls**, whether individually or in public preaching.

In conclusion of learning about Evangelists, and what defines them and their work, let us answer a few discovery questions.

Discovery Questions.

The answers to the following few questions might be telltale signs God anointed you as an Evangelist.

- Have you been able to lead people to Christ?
- Do you often find yourself sharing your faith with others in a way that move them to also accept Jesus as the Saviour and Lord?
- Do you often see people respond to the Gospel message when you deliver it?
- Do you find it naturally easy to share with people how to put their faith in Jesus?
- Do you often hear that people came to faith in Jesus Christ as a result of your sharing the Gospel Message?
- Do you find yourself daily looking for opportunities to share your faith and lead people to Christ?
- Do you have a strong sense that God anointed you with a special ability to lead people to salvation?
- Do people often ask you to come and share the Gospel Message with unbelievers?

If the answer to all of these statements is a strong *"YES"* then you probably have been anointed as an Evangelist. If the answer is more ***"YES, sometimes"*** then you should certainly open yourself up to the possibility that the Lord desire to increasingly use you to share your faith with others. If the answer is a ***"NO, I have never sensed such an urge or prompting beyond the occasional opportunity for me to share my faith,"*** then you might be one of those precious believers who has been blessed with some other prominent gift to serve the Body of Christ.

4. Pastor.

A **pastor** (literally, "**Shepherd**") is one who leads and takes care of God's people. The Greek word used, and only translated here as Pastor, is the Word **"poimen."** The other 16 times it is translated as "shepherd." The Bible also speaks of him as a bishop (literally, "Overseer") and an elder.

I Peter 5:1-4 describes the pastor's role of leading, overseeing, and instructing the believers under his care:

> **I Peter 5:1-4** *(NIV)*
> *"The elders who are among you I exhort, I who am a fellow elder and a witness of the sufferings of Christ, and also a partaker of the glory that will be revealed:* **Shepherd the flock of God which is among you,** *serving as overseers, not by constraint, but willingly, not for dishonest gain but eagerly; nor as being lords over those entrusted to you, but being examples to the flock; and when the Chief Shepherd appears, you will receive the crown of glory that does not fade away."*

The New Testament always speaks of elders in the plural, indicating that in each city the church was led by a pastoral team. Scripture, history, and common sense all indicate that there was a senior pastor or presiding elder.

Today we may think of the elders of the church in a city as the senior pastor and pastoral staff of a local church, or as the pastors of various congregations in one city who cooperate as part of the same organization.

The functions of a Pastor are likened unto that of being a Shepherd. We can learn more about these characteristics in John 10 where we read about the Great Shepherd and the heart with which He Shepherded His Sheep. **Ezekiel 34** also gives us an insight into the heart and operation of a Shepherd.

In conclusion of learning about Pastors, and what defines them and their work, let us answer a few discovery questions.

Discovery Questions.

The answers to the following few questions might be telltale signs that might help you to know whether you have been called and anointed as a Shepherd.

- Do you have a sense that God called and anointed you specifically to care for His people?
- Do you enjoy taking care of the spiritual and welfare needs of people?
- Do you feel more comfortable to work with people with whom you have well established relationships?
- Do you find yourself intentionally building deep and meaningful relationships with others so that you can care for them better?
- Do you often hear that people appreciate you for being there for them, and for taking good care of them?
- Do you have a deep sense that God gifted you to walk alongside, and to take care of people?
- Are you most fulfilled when you care for people in their most difficult situations?
- Do you find yourself giving Holy Spirit inspired messages and help to people in their difficulties?

If the answer to all of these statements is a strong *"YES"* then you most certainly have been called and anointed as a Pastor. If the answer is more "*YES, sometimes*" then you should certainly open yourself up to the possibility that the Lord desire to increasingly use you to take care of the needs and welfare of others. If the answer is a "*NO, I have never sensed such an urge or prompting,*" then you might be one of those precious believers who has been blessed with some other prominent gift to serve the Body of Christ.

5. Teacher.

A **teacher** is one who has been anointed and have special giftedness in bringing instruction in the Word of God. (Acts 13:1)

> *Acts 13:1 (NIV)*
> *[13:1] In the church at Antioch there were prophets and **teachers**: Barnabas, Simeon called Niger, Lucius of Cyrene, Manaen (who had been brought up with Herod the tetrarch) and Saul.*

As we have seen, in this context, and specifically in relation to these Spiritual Gifts in the Bible, the preaching and teaching roles are assigned to the overseers in the local church. While many people in the church may have the gift of teaching and can teach effectively in various settings, such as Sunday school classes and home Bible studies, the office of pastor-teacher stands above them. The pastor-teacher is the leading preacher and teacher of the Word. God has not only given him the gift of teaching, but God has given him to the church as its teacher and overseer.

In conclusion of learning about Teachers, and what defines them and their work, let us answer a few discovery questions.

Discovery Questions.

The answers to the following few questions might be telltale signs that will most certainly affirm that God called and anointed you as a Teacher to the body of Christ.

- Do you believe that God called and anointed you to be a Teacher of the Word of God?
- Do you enjoy teaching people in a systematic and understandable way the Truths of God's Word?
- Do you enjoy studying the Word and discovering new truths that you might be able to share?
- Do you frequently find yourself looking for new and innovative ways to communicate more efficiently the truths of God's Word?
- Do you feel honored to be able to see that, through your sharing the truths of God's Word, that fellow Believers grow in their faith?
- Do you have a strong urge to bring the truth to people to displace false beliefs and doctrines?
- Do you take delight, both in knowing the doctrines of the Bible, and by sharing them with others?
- Do you often receive compliments that you are a good teacher of the WORD OF GOD?

If the answer to all of these statements is a strong "**YES**" then you most certainly have been blessed by God in being gifted with the teaching gift as well as being given as a Gift from God to the Church. If the answer is more "**YES, sometimes**" then you should certainly open yourself up to the possibility that the Lord desire to increasingly use you to teach others through you. If the answer is a "**NO, I have never sensed such an urge or prompting,**" then you might be one of those precious believers who has been blessed with some other prominent gift to serve the Body of Christ.

What is the Purpose of these fivefold Ministry Gifts?

The purpose of the Ministerial Gifts is to equip and activate the Gifts of God in Believers.

Ephesians 4:12-16 (NIV)
*[12] **to prepare God's people for works of service, so that the body of Christ may be built up** [13] **until we all reach unity in the faith** and in the **knowledge of the Son of God** and **become mature**, attaining to the whole measure of the fullness of Christ. [14] Then we will no longer be infants, tossed back and forth by the waves, and blown here and there by every wind of teaching and by the cunning and craftiness of men in their deceitful scheming. [15] Instead, speaking the truth in love, we will in all things grow up into him who is the Head, that is, Christ. [16] From him the whole body, joined and held together by every supporting ligament, grows and builds itself up in love, as each part does its work.*

The Amplified Version expounds beautifully on the role and function of these Gifts God gave to the church.

Ephesians 4:12-16 (AMP)
*[12] **His intention was the perfecting and the full equipping of the saints (His consecrated people), [that they should do] the work of ministering toward building up Christ's body (the church),** [13] [That it might develop] until we all attain oneness in the faith and in the comprehension of the [full and accurate] knowledge of the Son of God, that [we might arrive] at really mature manhood (the completeness of personality which is nothing less than the standard height of Christ's own perfection), the measure of the stature of the fullness of the Christ and the completeness found in Him. [14] So then, we may no longer be children, tossed [like ships] to and fro between chance gusts of teaching and wavering with every changing wind of doctrine, [the prey of] the cunning and cleverness of unscrupulous men, [gamblers engaged] in every shifting form of trickery in inventing errors to mislead. [15] Rather, let our lives lovingly express truth [in all things, speaking truly, dealing truly, living truly]. Enfolded in love, let us grow up in every*

way and in all things into Him Who is the Head, [even] Christ (the Messiah, the Anointed One). [16] For because of Him the whole body (the church, in all its various parts), closely joined and firmly knit together by the joints and ligaments with which it is supplied, when each part [with power adapted to its need] is working properly [in all its functions], grows to full maturity, building itself up in love.

Verse 12 explains the purpose for which God gave apostles, prophets, evangelists, pastors and teachers to the church. The commas in this verse, in the KJV, could lead someone to interpret it as describing three separate tasks of these ministers, but punctuation was not part of the original text of Scripture. Translators added punctuation to aid in reading and for understanding. In this case, a study of the Greek text and various translations makes it clear that there is one purpose with a threefold progression, as follows:

- God gave the ministerial Gifts to the church for the "**perfecting**" (AMP) or "**equipping**" (NKJV) of the Believers.
- The Believers are equipped so they can do "**the work of ministry.**" Here, "**ministry**" means "**service,**" or all the functions of the church. **Every believer should have a ministry**—not necessarily a public preaching ministry but a specific place of service in the body of Christ. **It is the task of the apostles, prophets, evangelists, pastors and teachers to help each Believer to find their work of ministry** and **train them to perform that task properly** within the body. Those who hold the five ministerial offices are to *inspire, motivate, disciple, instruct, and prepare the Believers* so that **everyone become an active, productive member of the body.**
- When each member of the body performs his proper function, the whole body will be edified, or built up. The goal is to attain maturity in Christ. **Beginning** with "*the*

unity of the Spirit in the bond of peace" (Ephesians 4:3), we are to pursue "***the unity of the faith***" and "**the knowledge of the Son of God,**" to a perfect man, to the measure of the stature of the fullness of Christ" (Ephesians 4:13).

According to Ephesians 4:14-16, each local body of believers should seek everything God enabled them to have, that will characterize them as mature Believers:

- Becoming established in the faith so that they are not swayed by false doctrine and false leaders.
- Speaking the truth in love. They should learn to minister to one another and to unbelievers with a balance of honesty and compassion, equally valuing and manifesting truth and love.
- Submitting to the lordship of Jesus Christ in all things and depending upon His divine supply for all things.
- Everyone learning to contribute his or her share to the work of the church, so that the body can grow and be built up in love, using their Spiritual Gifts to build the Church up.

Summary

The ministerial office gifts of Ephesians chapter 4 are God's endowment to the local and worldwide church for the purpose of equipping the members for their assigned tasks. During the next session we will look at the service gifts of Romans 12, especially as to how God gives each member of the church one or more special abilities to help the church function productively as a body.

3

THE SERVICE GIFTS
SESSION THREE

The Service Gifts are those Supernatural Gifts, given to Believers, to enable them to perform and serve in extra-ordinary ways, and with extra-ordinary authority and ability.

Romans 12:3-8 (NIV)
*"For I say, through **the grace given to me**, to **everyone** who is among you, not to think of himself more highly than he ought to think, but to think soberly, as God has dealt to each one a measure of faith. For as we have many members in one body, but all the members do not have the same function, so we, being many, are one body in Christ, and individually members of one another. Having then gifts differing according to the grace that is given to us, let us use them: **if prophecy**, let us prophesy in proportion to our faith; **or ministry**, let us use it in our ministering; **he who teaches**, in teaching; **he who exhorts**, in exhortation; **he who gives**, with liberality; **he who leads**, with diligence; **he who shows mercy**, with cheerfulness"*

The Greek word for "gifts" here is *charismata*, the plural of *charisma*. It is also used of the nine spiritual gifts of I Corinthians 12. This word is related to *Charis*, or "grace," which refers to **the free, undeserved blessing and work of God**. The connotation is that these gifts are free, unmerited, miraculous endowments from God.

In this chapter, Paul cited seven avenues of his revelation of the service gifts. His manner of presentation reveals that the list of gifts here is **not exhaustive but representative or illustrative of the ways God uses individuals in His church**. There are many other aspects of Christian service that this passage does not specifically identify.

These are **truly giftings from God** and **not merely human attainments**. While there are some natural human abilities that correspond to this list, at least in part, even the talents we receive from birth, and those nurtured in us, have their ultimate source in the design, purpose, and grace of God.

In this session we will explore the following service gifts:

- Prophecy
- Serving
- Teaching
- Exhortation
- Giving
- Leading (ruling in KJV)
- Showing mercy

1. Prophecy.

The first in the list is prophecy, and it refers to a divinely inspired utterance, or speaking under divine unction to edify others. It refers specifically to a supernatural public message in the language of the audience.

> *Romans 12:6 (NIV)*
> *We have different gifts, according to the grace given us.* ***If a man's gift is prophesying, let him use it in proportion to his faith.***

It takes faith to prophecy, both since it requires faith to know that it was the voice of the Holy Spirit bringing the message to you, as well as speaking up to deliver the message in a way in which it will be heard and received with the right emphasis that the Holy Spirit delivered it to you.

The Greek word that is used is "*prophēteía*" and it describes the verb's meaning: "*to prophecy, prophesying; the gift of communicating and enforcing revealed truth.*"

The Strong's Concordance defines it as:

"4394 prophēteía (from 4396 /prophḗtēs, "prophet," which is derived from 4253/pró, "before" and 5346 /phēmí, "make clear, assert as a priority") properly, what is clarified beforehand; prophecy which involves divinely empowered forth-telling(asserting the mind of God) or foretelling (prediction) "[1]

The same word is used in the outlining of the 9 spiritual gifts and its subsequent use. I can only think that it has such prominence in the edification and upbuilding of the Body of Christ that Paul emphasised it in both of these compilations or summarizations of the Gifts.

From the Corinthians 14 text we are led to understand that we "*can all prophesy,*" or in my words "*bring encouraging and upbuilding messages,*" however, the further definition, that sets this use apart from the 1 Corinthians 12 reference is that here there is the injection of "*if someone comes with a revelation*" the other should retreat and allow preference to that kind of prophecy. I think that this later reference might refer to the "*level of faith*" that is required and applied in the use of the spiritual gift. In my understanding, at least for as far as what the same word is used, this service gift is the same spiritual gift of prophecy as explored in 1 Corinthians 12.

Some do explain, and even translate it, to reference more "the gift of preaching." I have to default to the Greek text. The Greek word for "*preaching*" is "*kérugma*" and there is no indication in the Greek that it is what Paul mentioned. He would have used *"kérugma"* instead of *"prophēteía"* if that is what he meant.

> *1 Corinthians 14:29-33 (NIV)*
> *[29] **Two or three prophets should speak**, and the others should weigh carefully what is said. [30] And if a revelation comes to someone who is sitting down, the first speaker should stop. [31] For **you can all prophesy** in turn **so that everyone may be instructed and encouraged**. [32] The spirits of prophets are subject to the control of prophets. [33] For God is not a God of disorder but of peace.*

As in this case it seems that these **"Prophets"** spoke **"without a revelation"** and would therefore be subject to those who truly bring a prophetic, forecasting message as a result of a divine revelation they received. It seems to indicate the more general prophetic use of anointed *"encouragement, godly instruction and guidance"* until someone has a *"revelation"* which should be regarded with greater respect.

> *Acts 2:17 (NIV)*
> *[17] "'In the last days, God says, I will pour out my Spirit on all people. **Your sons and daughters will prophesy**, your young men will see visions, your old men will dream dreams."*

> *1 Corinthians 14:3 (NIV)*
> *"[3] But **everyone who prophesies speaks to men for their strengthening, encouragement and comfort.**"*

If someone has this gift, he should exercise it in proportion to his faith—as much as his measure of faith will enable him. Speak the Word by faith, that it will change and transform those who hear and apply it in their lives. It requires faith to speak what you believe God is saying to you, and through you, to others.

Discover Questions.

In conclusion of learning about the Gift of Prophecy, and what defines it, let us answer a few discovery questions. The answers to the following few questions might be telltale signs that might help you to know whether you have received this gift.

- Do you delight in delivering encouraging messages from God to edify, exhort and comfort others?
- Do you often find encouraging messages, through your time in the Word and prayer, that you confidently share with others?
- Do you spontaneously sense that the Holy Spirit give you messages that will encourage and strengthen others?
- Do you often hear that prophetic messages you gave others, encouraged them, and brought great clarity and direction to what God wanted for them?
- Do you feel both blessed to be able to receive messages from God, as well as blessed to be able to confidently share them with others?

If the answer is a strong "**YES**" then you most certainly have been blessed by God in receiving the spiritual gift of prophecy to serve others. If the answer is more "**YES, sometimes**" then you should certainly open yourself up to the possibility that the Lord desire to increasingly use you to encourage and strengthen others through divinely inspired messages He delivers to you, and through you. If the answer is a "**NO, I have never sensed such an urge or prompting,**" then you might be one of those precious believers who has been blessed with some other prominent gift to serve the Body of Christ.

2. Serving

Serving means service to others, particularly service in the church. Some people *are especially gifted with an attitude and ability of service in certain capacities.* The Greek word is *diakonia*, which is a broad word that covers a variety of services, work, or assistance. It can also refer specifically to the work of a deacon, who helps with the business and organizational matters in a local church.

> *Romans 12:7 (NIV)*
> ***If it is serving, let him serve;*** *if it is teaching, let him teach;*

> *Acts 6:1-6 (NIV)*
> *[6:1] In those days when the number of disciples was increasing, the Grecian Jews among them complained against the Hebraic Jews because their widows were being overlooked in* ***the daily distribution of food.*** *[2] So the Twelve gathered all the disciples together and said, "**It would not be right for us to neglect the ministry of the word of God in order to wait on tables.** [3] Brothers, choose seven men from among you who are known to be full of the Spirit and wisdom.* ***We will turn this responsibility over to them*** *[4] and will give our attention to prayer and the ministry of the word." [5] This proposal pleased the whole group. They chose Stephen, a man full of faith and of the Holy Spirit; also, Philip, Procorus, Nicanor, Timon, Parmenas, and Nicolas from Antioch, a convert to Judaism. [6] They presented these men to the apostles, who prayed and laid their hands on them.*

What we learned from the Letter to Timothy is that those who serve as deacons in the local church should prove themselves as trustworthy and faithful stewards. The organized church has long benefitted from the sacrificial service of those operating in this gift.

> *1 Timothy 3:8-13 (NIV)*
> *Deacons, likewise, are to be men worthy of respect, sincere, not indulging in much wine, and not pursuing dishonest gain. [9] They must keep hold of the deep truths of the faith with a clear conscience. [10] They must first be tested; and then if there is*

nothing against them, let them serve as deacons. In the same way, their wives are to be women worthy of respect, not malicious talkers but temperate and trustworthy in everything. A deacon must be the husband of but one wife and must manage his children and his household well. [13] Those who have served well gain an excellent standing and great assurance in their faith in Christ Jesus.

Discovery Questions.

In conclusion of learning about the Gift of Serving, and what defines it, let us answer a few discovery questions. The answers to the following few questions might be telltale signs that might help you to know whether you have received this gift.

- Do you delight in doing ordinary tasks that make things easier for others?
- Do you enjoy being part of the team that set up and pack equipment away before and after church services?
- Do you enjoy making sure that facilities and things like dishes are clean so that others can enjoy a clean and safe environment?
- Do you find yourself always looking to do the little things that makes things easier for others?
- Do you actually prefer to do those behind the scenes things that make things go smoothly for those who serve up front and in front of others?
- Do you feel privileged to be able to serve and to help others fulfill their purpose?

If the answer to all of these statements is a strong "YES" then you most certainly have been blessed by God in receiving this spiritual gift to serve others. If the answer is more "YES, sometimes" then you should certainly open yourself up to the possibility that the Lord desire to increasingly use you to serve others through you. If the answer is a "NO, I have never sensed such an urge or prompting, then you might be one of those precious believers who has been blessed with some other prominent gift to serve the Body of Christ.

3. Teaching.

The gift of **teaching**, or the giving of instruction, is that gift of God by which others are taught in the truths of God's Word. House Group Leaders, Bible study group teachers, and Sunday school teachers are possible examples of people who operate in this gift. This is the gift of opening up something through teaching to someone, through the power of the Holy Spirit. This "opening up" is the gift in operation where you share some personal revelation or truth from the Word of God in a way that it is clearly understood, and where those receiving such teaching are inspired to put it into practice.

> *Romans 12:7 (NIV)*
> *If it is serving, let him serve; **if it is teaching, let him teach**;*

Definition:

The Greek word for Teacher is "***didaskalos.***" The Greek word for Teaching is "***didasko***". The Bible study tools define it as:

- to teach
- to hold discourse with others in order to instruct them, deliver didactic discourses
- to be a teacher
- to discharge the office of a teacher, conduct one's self as a teacher
- to teach one
- to impart instruction
- instill doctrine into one
- the thing taught or enjoined
- to explain or expound a thing

- to teach one something[2]

Jesus taught the people in the Synagogues and on the streets. We learn a lot about this spiritual gift by the way Jesus operated with it.

Mark 6:34 (NIV)
When Jesus landed and saw a large crowd, he had compassion on them, because they were like sheep without a shepherd. So, **he began teaching them many things.**

Jesus taught with authority and power. When someone flows in this gift, you will find that there is a level of authority and power on such teaching.

Luke 4:32 (NIV)
They were amazed at his teaching, *because his message* ***had authority.***

Luke 4:36 (NIV)
*All the people were amazed and said to each other, "****What is this teaching? With authority and power,*** *he gives orders to evil spirits and they come out!"*

Jesus taught us that His teaching came from above. A true teaching will carry with it a heavenly anointing of revelation and the spiritual eyes and hearts will be opened.

John 7:16-17 (NIV)
*16 Jesus answered, "****My teaching is not my own.*** *It comes from him who sent me. 17 If anyone chooses to do God's will, he will find out whether* ***my teaching comes from God*** *or whether I speak on my own."*

The Apostles practiced this gift everywhere they went. The things they taught became known as the Apostle's Teachings.

Acts 2:42 (NIV)
*They devoted themselves to the **apostles' teaching** and to the fellowship, to the breaking of bread and to prayer.*

Acts 5:28 (NIV)
*"We gave you strict orders not to teach in this name," he said. "Yet **you have filled Jerusalem with your teaching** and are determined to make us guilty of this man's blood."*

You have not taught someone until they have learned, and they have not learnt until you have taught them. The onus is on the teacher to ensure that the students learn. The fruit of this gift is that people learn truths when you teach it to them. You are able to communicate complex things in a simple and easy to understand way.

Acts 13 tells us that there were Teachers and Prophets fasting and praying together when the Holy Spirit spoke.

Acts 13:1 (NIV)
*In the church at Antioch there were prophets and **teachers**: Barnabas, Simeon called Niger, Lucius of Cyrene, Manaen (who had been brought up with Herod the tetrarch) and Saul.*

The Gracious intervention in making this gift active in our lives is the empowering that comes from the Holy Spirit, in allowing you to share His Instruction and Teaching in a way that allows others to be taught and be instructed. You know that God anointed you to teach His Word when you sense a strong willingness to be used by God to teach the truths of God's Word to others, and when you see how people assimilate the truths you share.

Discovery Questions.

In conclusion of learning about the Gift of Teaching, and what defines it, let us answer a few discovery questions. The answers to the following few questions might be telltale signs that might help you to know whether you have received this gift.

- Have you recently heard from Believers that they were greatly helped by the truths that you shared with them?
- Do you enjoy seeing people gain new insights when you share with them?
- Do you enjoy studying the Word and discovering new truths that you might be able to share?
- Do you frequently find yourself looking for new and innovative ways to communicate more efficiently the truths of God's Word?
- Do you feel honored to be able to see that, through your sharing the truths of God's Word, that fellow Believers grow in their faith?

If the answer to all of these statements is a strong "YES" then you most certainly have been blessed by God in receiving this spiritual gift to teach others. If the answer is more "YES, sometimes" then you should certainly open yourself up to the possibility that the Lord desire to increasingly use you to teach others through you. If the answer is a "NO, I have never sensed such an urge or prompting," then you might be one of those precious believers who has been blessed with some other prominent gift to serve the Body of Christ.

4. Exhortation.

Exhortation means to give encouragement or comfort. Some translations actually use encouraging and encourage instead of exhortation. *To exhort is to encourage.* Some people exercise this gift by public testimony, while others do so primarily by personal contact. Those who exercise this Gift often do so spontaneously with strangers, their friends or people they know who needs some cheering up. They exercise it in a variety of ways including naturally talking with people, telephone calls, letters, and cards.

> Romans 12:8 (NIV)
> "8 *if it is encouraging, let him encourage;* if it is contributing to the needs of others, let him give generously; if it is leadership, let him govern diligently; if it is showing mercy, let him do it cheerfully."

The Greek word is from the root word "**parakaleō**" which means "**to call to a person, to call to the side.**" To "**exhort**" is to come alongside someone.

Joseph was well-known for this gift that the apostles gave him the surname Barnabas, meaning "***Son of Encouragement.***"

> Acts 4:36-37 (NIV)
> [36] Joseph, a Levite from Cyprus, whom the apostles called **Barnabas (which means Son of Encouragement)**, [37] sold a field he owned and brought the money and put it at the apostles' feet.

Barnabas practiced this gift when he brought Paul to the Apostles. He walked alongside Paul until Paul was well established in his calling. Mentors often operate in this gifting as they pour courage and hope into protégés.

> Acts 9:26-27 (NIV)
> [26] When he came to Jerusalem, he tried to join the disciples, but they were all afraid of him, not believing that he really was a disciple. [27] But Barnabas took him and brought him to the apostles. He told them how Saul on his journey had seen the Lord and that the Lord had spoken to him, and how in Damascus he had preached fearlessly in the name of Jesus.

The Apostle operated in this gift when he spoke in the synagogue in Antioch on one of his visits.

Acts 13:15 (NIV)
After the reading from the Law and the Prophets, the synagogue rulers sent word to them, saying, "Brothers, if you have a message of encouragement for the people, please speak."

Paul seemed to operate in this gift quite a bit when he visited the region of Macedonia and Greece.

Acts 20:1-2 (NIV) Through Macedonia and Greece
*"1 When the uproar had ended, Paul sent for the disciples and, **after encouraging them**, said good-by and set out for Macedonia. 2 He traveled through that area, **speaking many words of encouragement to the people**, and finally arrived in Greece,"*

When we live united with Christ then we will always find ourselves encouraged.

Philippians 2:1 (NIV)
***"1 If you have any encouragement from being united with Christ,** if any comfort from his love, if any fellowship with the Spirit, if any tenderness and compassion,"*

Sometimes we find a brother or sister who just bring encouragement when they are with you.

Philemon 1:7 (NIV)
*"7 Your love has given me great joy and **encouragement**, because you, brother, have refreshed the hearts of the saints."*

Discovery Questions.

In conclusion of learning about the Gift of Exhortation, and what defines it, let us answer a few discovery questions. The answers to the following few questions might be telltale signs that might help you to know whether you have received this gift.

- Do you naturally and spontaneously see the positive side of sometimes difficult situations?
- Do you normally find some uplifting and positive thing to say to others?
- Do you daily make the effort to compliment people?
- Do you frequently hear that your positive attitude and words encourage others?
- Do you generally feel privileged that you have this positive ability to point people to the good and blessed things in life?

If the answer to all of these statements is a strong "**YES**" then you most certainly have been blessed by God in receiving this spiritual gift to bring encouragement and hope to others. If the answer is more "**YES, sometimes**" then you should certainly open yourself up to the possibility that the Lord desire to increasingly use you to exhort others through you. If the answer is a "**NO, I have never sensed such an urge or prompting**," then you might be one of those precious believers who has been blessed with some other prominent gift to serve the Body of Christ.

5. Gift of Giving.

The **gift of giving is sharing material blessings with the church and with others.**

> *Romans 12:8 AMP*
> "He who exhorts (encourages), to his exhortation; **he who**

contributes, let him do it in simplicity and liberality; he who gives aid and superintends, with zeal and singleness of mind; he who does acts of mercy, with genuine cheerfulness and joyful eagerness."

The Amplified Bible (**AMP**) says to give with "**simplicity,**" but most commentators understand the underlying Greek word to mean "**liberally, and generously.**" It can also mean "**singleness of heart, sincere concern.**" Some people are blessed significantly more than others with the means and opportunity to give to God's cause.

> 1 Timothy 6:17-20 (NIV) 17 Command those who are rich in this present world not to be arrogant nor to put their hope in wealth, which is so uncertain, but to put their hope in God, who richly provides us with everything for our enjoyment. 18 Command them to do good, to be rich in good deeds, and to be generous and willing to share. 19 In this way they will lay up treasure for themselves as a firm foundation for the coming age, so that they may take hold of the life that is truly life.

They **should not consider** their material blessings to be **a sign of superiority** but **a gift of God for the purpose of assisting His kingdom in a special way.** They should not be selfish but generous, recognizing that in God's plan they have greater ability and responsibility to give than most others.

> 2 Corinthians 9:10-11 (NIV) 10 Now he who supplies seed to the sower and bread for food will also supply and increase your store of seed and will enlarge the harvest of your righteousness. 11 You will be enriched in every way so that you can be generous on every occasion, and through us your generosity will result in thanksgiving to God.

Discovery Questions.

In conclusion of learning about the Gift of Giving, and what defines it, let us answer a few discovery questions. The answers to the following few questions might be telltale signs that might help you to know whether you have received this gift.

- Are you quite disciplined in managing your finances?
- Are your finances in a state where you generally are able to give generously to the Lord's work?
- Do your financial records show that you are able to give more than just your tithe?
- Are you often approached to give to some Kingdom advancing cause?
- Are you able to give generously when requests are made to give?
- Do you often find yourself, even when you are stretched, giving, just because you believe in a cause, and because you love to see God's work advance?
- Do often revisit your budget to see where you are able to reduce expenses to enable you to do more for the advance of the Kingdom of God?

If the answer to all of these statements is a strong "**YES**" then you most certainly have been blessed by God in receiving this spiritual gift to be a generous giver. If the answer is more "**YES, sometimes**" then you should certainly open yourself up to the possibility that the Lord desire to increasingly use you to give so that others may be blessed through your giving and support. If the answer is a "**NO, I have never sensed such an urge or prompting**," then you might be one of those precious believers who has been blessed with some other prominent gift to serve the Body of Christ.

6. Gift of Leadership.

Leading, or ruling in the KJV, speaks of direction, guidance, and influence within the church. Leaders are to exercise their role with diligence, carefulness, and earnestness. God has ordained rulers or leaders in His church.

The Greek word gives beautiful expression of it meaning. The Greek word is "**proistēmi**" and means "*to put before, to set over and to rule.*" With diligence which is the word "*spoudē*" and where we get our English word "*expedient*" from (***to be diligent and earnest in effort.***)

> *Romans 12:8 (NIV)*
> *8 if it is encouraging, let him encourage; if it is contributing to the needs of others, let him give generously;* ***if it is leadership, let him govern diligently;*** *if it is showing mercy, let him do it cheerfully.*

It is important to submit to human authority in the church, as long as human leaders exercise their authority under God according to the guidelines of His Word.

> *Hebrews 13:17 (NIV)*
> *17 Have confidence in your leaders and submit to their authority, because they keep watch over you as those who must give an account. Do this so that their work will be a joy, not a burden, for that would be of no benefit to you.*

The church needs various people with leadership and administrative ability. In addition to the pastor and pastoral staff, the successful congregation will have capable leaders over various departments and activities as well as influential opinion makers and role models who may or may not have an official position.

Discovery Questions.

In conclusion of learning about the Gift of Leadership, and what defines it, let us answer a few discovery questions. The answers to the following few questions might be telltale signs that might help you to know whether you have received this gift.

- Do you find that others easily follow the decisions you make?
- Do you find that people often look to you for guidance and direction in what to do?
- Do people often ask you what to do next?
- Do you find that people naturally follow the ideas and suggestions you propose?
- Do you feel that you have been blessed to make thought-through decisions?

If the answer to all of these statements is a strong "**YES**" then you most certainly have been blessed by God in receiving this spiritual gift to lead others. If the answer is more "**YES, sometimes**" then you should certainly open yourself up to the possibility that the Lord desire to increasingly use you to lead others. If the answer is a "**NO, I have never sensed such an urge or prompting,**" then you might be one of those precious believers who has been blessed with some other prominent gift to serve the Body of Christ.

7. Showing Mercy.

Showing mercy means **being merciful and kind to others**. It can include visiting the sick, helping the poor, and assisting widows and orphans.

Romans 12:8 (NIV)
if it is encouraging, let him encourage; if it is contributing to the needs of others, let him give generously; if it is leadership, let

*him govern diligently; **if it is showing mercy, let him do it cheerfully.***

Matthew 25:31-40 (NIV) The Sheep and the Goats
[31] "When the Son of Man comes in his glory, and all the angels with him, he will sit on his throne in heavenly glory. [32] All the nations will be gathered before him, and he will separate the people one from another as a shepherd separates the sheep from the goats. [33] He will put the sheep on his right and the goats on his left. [34] "Then the King will say to those on his right, 'Come, you who are blessed by my Father; take your inheritance, the kingdom prepared for you since the creation of the world. [35] For I was hungry and you gave me something to eat, I was thirsty and you gave me something to drink, I was a stranger and you invited me in, [36] I needed clothes and you clothed me, I was sick and you looked after me, I was in prison and you came to visit me.' [37] "Then the righteous will answer him, 'Lord, when did we see you hungry and feed you, or thirsty and give you something to drink? [38] When did we see you a stranger and invite you in, or needing clothes and clothe you? [39] When did we see you sick or in prison and go to visit you?' [40] "The King will reply, 'I tell you the truth, whatever you did for one of the least of these brothers of mine, you did for me.'

Galatians 2:10 (NIV)
[10] All they asked was that we should continue to remember the poor, the very thing I was eager to do.

James 1:27 (NIV)
[27] Religion that God our Father accepts as pure and faultless is this: to look after orphans and widows in their distress and to keep oneself from being polluted by the world.

James 2:15-17 (NIV)
[15] Suppose a brother or sister is without clothes and daily food. [16] If one of you says to him, "Go, I wish you well; keep warm and well fed," but does nothing about his physical needs, what good is it? [17] In the same way, faith by itself, if it is not accompanied by action, is dead.

A person who fills this role should do it cheerfully, not in a begrudging, mournful, or patronizing way. To some extent, every mature Christian should be able to function in the seven areas just listed. **All Christians are to be** *an effective witness*, **to serve, to encourage, to give,** and **to show mercy.** All should have **some basic ability to instruct unbelievers in the plan of salvation and to lead new converts in the ways of the Lord.**

This passage tells us, however, that each Christian has some area of special strength, given by God. While we should always "**be ready for every good work**" (Titus 3:1), we need to discern what our strong points are and use them effectively.

Discovery Questions.

In conclusion of learning about the Gift of Mercy, and what defines it, let us answer a few discovery questions. The answers to the following few questions might be telltale signs that might help you to know whether you have received this gift.

- Do you prefer working and assisting people who find themselves physically and mentally challenged?
- Do you often and naturally find yourself taking care of those with material and physical needs?
- People often call on me to make hospital visits.
- Do you frequently get asked to visit those in troublesome circumstances?
- Do you love walking alongside people to help them find solutions to their problems?

- Do you feel blessed to be able to have the temperament to help those in physical, mental and material challenging situations?

If the answer to all of these statements is a strong "**YES**" then you most certainly have been blessed by God in receiving this spiritual gift to show Mercy others. If the answer is more "**YES, sometimes**" then you should certainly open yourself up to the possibility that the Lord desire to increasingly use you to extend and show Mercy to others. If the answer is a "**NO, I have never sensed such an urge or prompting,**" then you might be one of those precious believers who has been blessed with some other prominent gift to serve the Body of Christ.

Afterword

To summarize, each Christian is part of the Body, the Body of Christ that is, and has a particular gift, role, or function in the church, or possibly several of them. Whatever God has given him to do; he should exercise it to his full capacity but always with humility.

Being a Christian means being a part of a body. Understanding where God, the creator and developer of the Body placed you, will bring you to a place of understanding your purpose, and finding fulfillment.

4

THE SUPERNATURAL SPIRITUAL GIFTS
SESSION FOUR

In this session we will look, and explore, the Supernatural Spiritual Gifts.

The Supernatural Spiritual Gifts are primarily defined in 1 Corinthians chapter 12.

> *1 Corinthians 12:7-11 (NIV)*
>
> *[7] Now to each one the manifestation of the Spirit is given for the common good. [8] To one there is given through the Spirit the message of wisdom, to another the message of knowledge by means of the same Spirit, [9] to another faith by the same Spirit, to another gifts of healing by that one Spirit, [10] to another miraculous powers, to another prophecy, to another distinguishing between spirits, to another speaking in different kinds of tongues,* and to still another the interpretation of tongues.* [11] All these are the work of one and the same Spirit, and he gives them to each one, just as he determines.*

The Supernatural Spiritual Gifts are:

We recognize nine Gifts in this portion of Scripture. They are:

- Word of Wisdom
- Word of Knowledge
- Faith
- Gifts of healings
- Working of miracles
- Prophecy
- Discerning of spirits
- Different kinds of tongues
- Interpretation of tongues

1. Words of Wisdom

A Word of Wisdom is characterized by it being wise counsel and guidance within a specified situation. The Wisdom that the Holy Spirit will reveal, will bring clarity, soundness and practical application within a known situation. It will answer the "How to" and "what must I do" in a given circumstance that you are facing.

> *1 Corinthians 2:6-8 (NIV)*
> **6 We do, however, speak a message of wisdom** *among the mature, but not the wisdom of this age or of the rulers of this age, who are coming to nothing. 7. No,* **we declare God's wisdom, a mystery that has been hidden and that God destined for our glory before time began.** *8. None of the rulers of this age understood it, for if they had, they would not have crucified the Lord of glory.*

In this Scripture reference we see this Gift of Words of Wisdom in operation. We bring messages that in essence brings Supernatural Wisdom, not naturally known. As we see in another example in Acts chapter six, that when this Gift is in operation, it is hard to stand up against its soundness and clarity.

> Acts 6:3,10 (NIV)
> 3 Brothers and sisters, choose seven men from among you who are **known to be full of the Spirit and wisdom.** We will turn this responsibility over to them. 10 But they could not stand up against **the wisdom the Spirit gave** him as he spoke.

The Apostle Paul expounds on How this Gift brings revelation of things not previously known.

> I Corinthians 2:1-13 (NIV)
> ¹And so it was with me, brothers and sisters. When I came to you, I did not come with eloquence or human wisdom as I proclaimed to you the testimony about God. I came to you in weakness with great fear and trembling. My message and my preaching were not with wise and persuasive words, but with a demonstration of the Spirit's power, so that your faith might not rest on human wisdom, but on God's power. We do, however, speak a message of wisdom among the mature, but not the wisdom of this age or of the rulers of this age, who are coming to nothing. No, we declare God's wisdom, a mystery that has been hidden and that God destined for our glory before time began. None of the rulers of this age understood it, for if they had, they would not have crucified the Lord of glory. However, as it is written: "What no eye has seen, what no ear has heard, and what no human mind has conceived" — the things God has prepared for those who love him— these are the things God has revealed to us by his Spirit. The Spirit searches all things, even the deep things of God. What we have received is not the spirit of the world, but the Spirit who is from God, so that we may understand what God has freely given us. This is what we speak, not in words taught us by human wisdom but in words taught by the Spirit,

explaining spiritual realities with Spirit-taught words. For who knows a person's thoughts except their own spirit within them? In the same way no one knows the thoughts of God except the Spirit of God. For I resolved to know nothing while I was with you except Jesus Christ and him crucified.'

We receive these Words of Wisdom by the Holy Spirit. This Wisdom is not acquired in natural ways, we receive it by divine revelation from the Holy Spirit.

I Corinthians 12:8 (NIV)
'To one there is given through the Spirit a message of wisdom, to another a message of knowledge by means of the same Spirit,'

One way in which we can receive this Gift is to ask God for it. The Apostle James exhorts us who lack wisdom to go to God and to ask Him for wisdom.

James 1:5,6 (NIV)
'If any of you lacks wisdom, you should ask God, who gives generously to all without finding fault, and it will be given to you. But when you ask, you must believe and not doubt, because the one who doubts is like a wave of the sea, blown and tossed by the wind.'

It is clear from the Apostle Peter's second letter that the Apostle Paul wrote Words of Wisdom that He received from God.

2 Peter 3:15,16 (NIV)
15 Bear in mind that our Lord's patience means salvation, just as our dear brother Paul also wrote you with the wisdom that God gave him. He writes the same way in all his letters, speaking in them of these matters. 16 His letters contain some things that are hard to understand, which ignorant and unstable people distort, as they do the other Scriptures, to their own destruction.

Discovery Questions.

The answers to the following few questions might be telltale signs that might help you to know whether you have received this gift.

- Do you find it easy to apply biblical principles, in context, in your life?
- Do you often find yourself coming up with solutions to fairly complicated situations?
- Do you frequently find yourself helping believers find solutions and answers through biblical examples and stories?
- Do you often hear that the Biblical Truth you share is most relevant and specific to felt needs?
- Do you have a sense of deep peace and personal confidence when you need to make important decisions?

If the answer to all of these statements is a strong "**YES**" then you most certainly have been blessed by God in receiving the spiritual gift of Wisdom to help and guide others. If the answer is more "**YES, sometimes**" then you should certainly open yourself up to the possibility that the Lord desire to increasingly use you to help and guide others through the wisdom He gave to you. If the answer is a "**NO, I have never sensed such an urge or prompting,**" then you might be one of those precious believers who has been blessed with some other prominent gift to serve the Body of Christ.

2. Words of Knowledge

A Word of Knowledge is characterized by knowledge being Supernaturally revealed to a Believer who had no prior knowledge or insight into the revealed details. Jesus and many Believers subsequently experienced the operation of this extra-ordinary gift.

We read of one prominent example, of this Gift in operation, in Acts chapter five where the Holy Spirit reveals knowledge about a transaction that took place, and a devised scheme, to lie about the proceeds of the sale.

> *Acts 5:1-11(NIV) Ananias and Sapphira*
> *'Now a man named Ananias, together with his wife Sapphira, also sold a piece of property. With his wife's full knowledge, he kept back part of the money for himself, but brought the rest and put it at the apostles' feet. Then Peter said, "Ananias, how is it that Satan has so filled your heart that you have lied to the Holy Spirit and have kept for yourself some of the money you received for the land? Didn't it belong to you before it was sold? And after it was sold, wasn't the money at your disposal? What made you think of doing such a thing? You have not lied just to human beings but to God." When Ananias heard this, he fell down and died. And great fear seized all who heard what had happened. Then some young men came forward, wrapped up his body, and carried him out and buried him. About three hours later his wife came in, not knowing what had happened. Peter asked her, "Tell me, is this the price you and Ananias got for the land?" "Yes," she said, "that is the price." Peter said to her, "How could you conspire to test the Spirit of the Lord? Listen! The feet of the men who buried your husband are at the door, and they will carry you out also." At that moment she fell down at his feet and died. Then the young men came in and, finding her dead, carried her out and buried her beside her husband. Great fear seized the whole church and all who heard about these events.'*

A few Gifts of the Holy Spirit was in operation here. The results of their scheming was disastrous.

It is mind-blowing how the Holy Spirit is able to bring knowledge to a person. This can only be understood, and received, by those who enjoy the indwelling of the Holy Spirit.

I Corinthians 2:14 (NIV)
'The person without the Spirit does not accept the things that come from the Spirit of God but considers them foolishness and cannot understand them because they are discerned only through the Spirit.'

We receive this Gift from the Holy Spirit.

1 Corinthians 12:8 (NIV)
*'To one there is given through the Spirit a message of wisdom, to another **a message of knowledge** by means of the same Spirit,'*

The "Knowledge" Paul refers to, in his second letter to the church in Corinthians, as well as his address to the church in Colossea, is this Gift of Knowledge.

2 Corinthians 11:6 (NIV)
*'I may indeed be untrained as a speaker, but **I do have knowledge**. We have made this perfectly clear to you in every way.'*

Colossians 2:2,3 (NIV)
'My goal is that they may be encouraged in heart and united in love, so that they may have the full riches of complete understanding, in order that they may know the mystery of God, namely, Christ, in whom are hidden all the treasures of wisdom and knowledge.'

I pray that many of you will be filled with this kind of Supernatural Knowledge, and that through its operation and use in our lives that the wisdom of God will be shared and many give praise to God.

Discovery Questions.

The answers to the following few questions might be telltale signs that might help you to know whether you have received this gift.

- Do you frequently find that the Holy Spirit give you insight into people's lives without any prior knowledge of them and their circumstances?
- Do you often find that you have knowledge about people, their children, their work, their personality, their present circumstances, without having any prior knowledge of them?
- Do you find yourself at times knowing people's names, place names, conditions in people, without ever learning it or being introduced to them?
- Do you often receive and share insight into the spiritual situations of people, and then consequently see how it brought them closer to God?
- Do you often find new strategies and techniques from studying the Scriptures that you eventually see help further the Kingdom of God?
- Do you frequently find yourself praying to understand what God desires to say to His people, that lines up with the Word?
- Do you often find that the Holy Spirit gives you first-hand knowledge and insight about situations?

If the answer to all of these statements is a strong "**YES**" then you most certainly have been blessed by God in receiving this spiritual gift of Knowledge. If the answer is more "**YES, sometimes**" then you should certainly open yourself up to the possibility that the Lord desire to increasingly use you to encourage others, or to bring insight into specific situations and circumstances. If the answer is a "**NO, I have never sensed such an urge or prompting,**" then you might be one of those precious believers who has been blessed with some other prominent gift to serve the Body of Christ.

3. Faith

The Gift of Faith is seen in operation when extra-ordinary faith is demonstrated as to show the Power and Greatness of God.

> *Acts 11:22-24 (NIV)*
> *'News of this reached the church in Jerusalem, and they sent Barnabas to Antioch. When he arrived and saw what the grace of God had done, he was glad and encouraged them all to remain true to the Lord with all their hearts. He was a good man, full of the Holy Spirit and faith, and a great number of people were brought to the Lord.'*

The Apostles constantly walked in this Gift of Faith.

> *Acts 27:21-25(NIV)*
> *'After they had gone a long time without food, Paul stood up before them and said: "Men, you should have taken my advice not to sail from Crete; then you would have spared yourselves this damage and loss. But now I urge you to keep up your courage, because not one of you will be lost; only the ship will be destroyed. Last night an angel of the God to whom I belong and whom I serve stood beside me and said, 'Do not be afraid, Paul. You must stand trial before Caesar; and God has graciously given you the lives of all who sail with you.' So keep up your courage, men, for I have faith in God that it will happen just as he told me.'*

As we can see here again, a number of Gifts operate together. Faith rises in our hearts and God fills us with courage to accomplish the almost impossible when we act on His Words.

Abraham - the Father of Faith

Father Abraham was such a Man of Faith. He was known as the Father of Faith due to him walking in this kind of Supernatural Faith.

> Romans 4:18-21 (NIV)
> 'Against all hope, Abraham in hope believed and so became the father of many nations, just as it had been said to him, "So shall your offspring be." Without weakening in his faith, he faced the fact that his body was as good as dead—since he was about a hundred years old—and that Sarah's womb was also dead. Yet he did not waver through unbelief regarding the promise of God, but was strengthened in his faith and gave glory to God, being fully persuaded that God had power to do what he had promised.'

We receive this Faith from the Holy Spirit.

> I Corinthians 12:9 (NIV) 'to another faith by the same Spirit, to another gifts of healing by that one Spirit,'

Hebrews 11 is an entire chapter devoted to people who practiced their Faith.

Discovery Questions.

The answers to the following few questions might be telltale signs that might help you to know whether you have received this gift.

- Do you find it easy to trust God when He gives you new assignments?
- Do you often find yourself doing things and taking on things that has not been attempted or done before, simply since you sensed the leading of the Holy Spirit in it?

- Do you frequently find yourself stepping out in faith to do things?
- Do you frequently hear how people admire you for the boldness they observe, which you apply, to advance the Kingdom of God?
- Do you feel confident to do things when you have a strong sense of personal conviction?

If the answer to all of these statements is a strong "**YES**" then you most certainly have been blessed by God in receiving the spiritual gift of Faith. If the answer is more "**YES, sometimes**" then you should certainly open yourself up to the possibility that the Lord desire to increasingly use you to advance His work by applying the Gift of Faith. If the answer is a "**NO, I have never sensed such an urge or prompting,**" then you might be one of those precious believers who has been blessed with some other prominent gift to serve the Body of Christ.

4. Gifts of Healing

The Gift of Healing is seen in operation when Believers are moved to lay their hands on sick people and they receive their healing in a supernatural way.

The Apostles operated in this Gift quite frequently. One such occasion was when Peter and John healed the Cripple man at the Gate Beautiful.

Acts 3:1-10 (NIV)
'One day Peter and John were going up to the temple at the time of prayer—at three in the afternoon. Now a man who was lame from birth was being carried to the temple gate called Beautiful, where he was put every day to beg from those going into the temple courts. When he saw Peter and John about to enter, he asked them for money. Peter looked straight at him, as did John. Then Peter said, "Look at us!" So the man gave them his

> *attention, expecting to get something from them. Then Peter said, "Silver or gold I do not have, but what I do have I give you. In the name of Jesus Christ of Nazareth, walk." Taking him by the right hand, he helped him up, and instantly the man's feet and ankles became strong. He jumped to his feet and began to walk. Then he went with them into the temple courts, walking and jumping, and praising God. When all the people saw him walking and praising God, they recognized him as the same man who used to sit begging at the temple gate called Beautiful, and they were filled with wonder and amazement at what had happened to him.'*

It is so much easier to simply to just highlight the one or two verse that jump out at us, however, I pray that by going through the whole portions we catch the Spirit of it to its fullest extent.

Another example of How these Apostles walked in this Gift on a daily basis is seen in Acts chapter five. The Bible says that the Apostles "performed many signs and wonders."

Acts 5:12-16 (NIV)
> *'The apostles performed many signs and wonders among the people. And all the believers used to meet together in Solomon's Colonnade. No one else dared join them, even though they were highly regarded by the people. Nevertheless, more and more men and women believed in the Lord and were added to their number. As a result, people brought the sick into the streets and laid them on beds and mats so that at least Peter's shadow might fall on some of them as he passed by. Crowds gathered also from the towns around Jerusalem, bringing their sick and those tormented by impure spirits, and all of them were healed.'*

The result of these signs and wonders and miraculous Healing was that many came to the Lord.

Acts 9:32-35 (NIV)

> 'As Peter traveled about the country, he went to visit the Lord's people who lived in Lydda. There he found a man named Aeneas, who was paralyzed and had been bedridden for eight years. "Aeneas," Peter said to him, "Jesus Christ heals you. Get up and roll up your mat." Immediately Aeneas got up. All those who lived in Lydda and Sharon saw him and turned to the Lord.'

> Acts 28:7-10 (NIV) 'There was an estate nearby that belonged to Publius, the chief official of the island. He welcomed us to his home and showed us generous hospitality for three days. His father was sick in bed, suffering from fever and dysentery. Paul went in to see him and, after prayer, placed his hands on him and healed him. When this had happened, the rest of the sick on the island came and were cured. They honored us in many ways; and when we were ready to sail, they furnished us with the supplies we needed.'

We receive this Gift to Heal the sick and to perform miracles from the Holy Spirit.

> *I Corinthians 12:9,28 (NIV)*
> '9 to another faith by the same Spirit, to another gifts of healing by that one Spirit, 28 And God has placed in the church first of all apostles, second prophets, third teachers, then miracles, then gifts of healing, of helping, of guidance, and of different kinds of tongues.'

Discovery Questions.

The answers to the following few questions might be telltale signs that might help you to know whether you have received this gift.

- I have been used by God to pray for the sick and they received their healing?

- Do you see people who suffer from spiritual and mental unwellness healed under your prayers?
- Do you often see instantaneous healings under your ministry?
- Do you frequently find people giving praise to God for healing them when you prayed for them?
- Do you frequently have a sense that the Lord want to heal people in your ministry, and then, when you pray for them, they receive their healing?

If the answer to all of these statements is a strong "**YES**" then you most certainly have been blessed by God in receiving this spiritual gift of Healing. If the answer is more "**YES, sometimes**" then you should certainly open yourself up to the possibility that the Lord desire to increasingly use you to Heal others. If the answer is a "**NO, I have never sensed such an urge or prompting**," then you might be one of those precious believers who has been blessed with some other prominent gift to serve the Body of Christ.

5. Working of Miracles

The Working of Miracles is seen in operation when Believers perform miracles in an extra-ordinary way under the influence of the Holy Spirit.

Raising someone from the dead is impossible in the natural unless God performs such a miracle, such as was the case with Tabitha.

> *Acts 9:36-42 (NIV) In Joppa there was a disciple named Tabitha (in Greek her name is Dorcas); she was always doing good and helping the poor. About that time, she became sick and died, and her body was washed and placed in an upstairs room. Lydda was near Joppa; so, when the disciples heard that Peter was in Lydda, they sent two men to him and urged him, "Please come at once!" Peter went with them, and when he arrived, he was*

> taken upstairs to the room. All the widows stood around him, crying and showing him the robes and other clothing that Dorcas had made while she was still with them. Peter sent them all out of the room; then he got down on his knees and prayed. Turning toward the dead woman, he said, "Tabitha, get up." She opened her eyes and seeing Peter she sat up. He took her by the hand and helped her to her feet. Then he called for the believers, especially the widows, and presented her to them alive. This became known all over Joppa, and many people believed in the Lord.

We see the most incredible miracles take place when we open ourselves up to the powerful work of the Holy Spirit. Paul experienced this "extraordinary miracles" wherever he went to preach the Gospel.

> *Acts 19:11-12 (NIV)*
> 'God did extraordinary miracles through Paul, so that even handkerchiefs and aprons that had touched him were taken to the sick, and their illnesses were cured, and the evil spirits left them.'

Paul raised a young boy to life in Acts chapter twenty.

> *Acts 20:7-12 (NIV)*
> 'On the first day of the week we came together to break bread. Paul spoke to the people and, because he intended to leave the next day, kept on talking until midnight. There were many lamps in the upstairs room where we were meeting. Seated in a window was a young man named Eutychus, who was sinking into a deep sleep as Paul talked on and on. When he was sound asleep, he fell to the ground from the third story and was picked up dead. Paul went down, threw himself on the young man and put his arms around him. "Don't be alarmed," he said. "He's alive!" Then he went upstairs again and broke bread and ate.

> *After talking until daylight, he left. The people took the young man home alive and were greatly comforted.'*

Paul declared that is was by the Power of the Holy Spirit that he was able to perform all the miracles.

> *Romans 15:18-19 (NIV)*
> *"18 I will not venture to speak of anything except what Christ has accomplished through me in leading the Gentiles to obey God by what I have said and done—19 by the power of signs and wonders, through the power of the Spirit of God. So from Jerusalem all the way around to Illyricum, I have fully proclaimed the gospel of Christ."*

> *1 Corinthians 12:10,28 (NIV)*
> *"10 to another miraculous powers, to another prophecy, to another distinguishing between spirits, to another speaking in different kinds of tongues, and to still another the interpretation of tongues. 28 And God has placed in the church first of all apostles, second prophets, third teachers, then miracles, then gifts of healing, of helping, of guidance, and of different kinds of tongues."*

One of the distinctive signs of an Apostle is that flow in this Gift of the Working of Miracles.

> *2 Corinthians 12:12 (NIV)*
> *"12 I persevered in demonstrating among you the marks of a true apostle, including signs, wonders and miracles."*

Discovery Questions.

The answers to the following few questions might be telltale signs that might help you to know whether you have received this gift.

- Do you see extra-ordinary miracles take place when you pray?
- Do you often see demon spirits come out of people when you minister to them?
- Do you frequently find yourself pray for impossible things to become possible, and then it happens just as you prayed?
- Do you frequently find that things you declared and prayed for, come true just as you declared?
- Do you often see blind eyes open and deaf ears open when you pray for them?

If the answer to all of these statements is a strong "**YES**" then you most certainly have been blessed by God in receiving the spiritual gift of working Miracles. If the answer is more "**YES, sometimes**" then you should certainly open yourself up to the possibility that the Lord desire to increasingly use you to perform mighty miracles through you. If the answer is a "**NO, I have never sensed such an urge or prompting**," then you might be one of those precious believers who has been blessed with some other prominent gift to serve the Body of Christ.

6. Prophecy

The Gift of Prophecy, as is often only explored here, was explained in the previous session. This gift is experienced when a Believer bring a revelation of some future activity, event or happening through the enablement of the Holy Spirit, and it consistently happens just as it was prophesied.

7. Discerning of Spirits

The Gift of Discerning of spirits is experienced when a Believer come to accurately discern differing spirits. This proves especially helpful in discerning opposing spirits.

> *Luke 4:33-35 (NIV)*
>
> *33 In the synagogue there was a man possessed by a demon, an impure spirit. He cried out at the top of his voice, 34 Go away! What do you want with us, Jesus of Nazareth? Have you come to destroy us? I know who you are —the Holy One of God! 35 Be quiet!" Jesus said sternly. "Come out of him!" Then the demon threw the man down before them all and came out without injuring him."*

> *Acts 16:16-18 (NIV) Paul and Silas in Prison*
>
> *"16 Once when we were going to the place of prayer, we were met by a female slave who had a spirit by which she predicted the future. She earned a great deal of money for her owners by fortune-telling. 17 She followed Paul and the rest of us, shouting, "These men are servants of the Most High God, who are telling you the way to be saved." 18 She kept this up for many days. Finally, Paul became so annoyed that he turned around and said to the spirit, "In the name of Jesus Christ I command you to come out of her!" At that moment the spirit left her."*

We need the discerning of spirits so much more in the day that we are living in. For a powerful ministry we need to discern the spirit within a man, and if needed, cast it out. I believe that there are more people tormented by evil spirits than what we give attention to. Jesus amounted us to have power over all the power of the evil one, and to cast out demons.

> *I Corinthians 12:10 (NIV)*
>
> *"10 to another miraculous powers, to another prophecy, to another distinguishing between spirits, to another speaking in different kinds of tongues, and to still another the interpretation of tongues."*

May we walk in this discernment daily. I pray that we will have a zeal and desire to have this Gift, to see the captives set free around us.

I John 4:1-6 (NIV)
"1 Dear friends, do not believe every spirit, but test the spirits to see whether they are from God, because many false prophets have gone out into the world. 2 This is how you can recognize the Spirit of God: Every spirit that acknowledges that Jesus Christ has come in the flesh is from God, 3 but every spirit that does not acknowledge Jesus is not from God. This is the spirit of the antichrist, which you have heard is coming and even now is already in the world. 4 You, dear children, are from God and have overcome them, because the one who is in you is greater than the one who is in the world. 5 They are from the world and therefore speak from the viewpoint of the world, and the world listens to them. 6 We are from God, and whoever knows God listens to us; but whoever is not from God does not listen to us. This is how we recognize the Spirit of truth and the spirit of falsehood."

Discovery Questions.

The answers to the following few questions might be telltale signs that might help you to know whether you have received this gift.

- Do you often find yourself seeing through the pretences of people, especially before it is evident to other people?
- Do you often see the specific Call and Purpose of God on people?
- Do you have a strong sense of assurance to discern when a person is afflicted by an evil spirit?
- Do you quickly discern whether a teaching is from God, Satan or from a person himself?
- Do you easily tell whether a person speaking in tongues is bringing a divine message, merely praying in the Spirit, or faking it?

If the answer to all of these statements is a strong "**YES**" then you most certainly have been blessed by God in receiving this spiritual gift of Discerning of Spirits. If the answer is more "**YES, sometimes**" then you should certainly open yourself up to the possibility that the Lord desire to increasingly use you to discern the spirits in a place and in people. If the answer is a "**NO, I have never sensed such an urge or prompting,**" then you might be one of those precious believers who has been blessed with some other prominent gift to serve the Body of Christ.

8. The Gift of Tongues

The Gift of Tongues is the ability to speak in a language, not learned, but received from the Holy Spirit when you received the baptism of the Holy Spirit. The Gift of tongues is a supernatural ability to bring messages from God to His people in a language that is not necessarily understood in the natural. We can use the gift of tongues to communicate, with the help of the Holy Spirit within us, to the Father in an inexplicable way.

> *Mark 16:17 (NIV)*
> *"17 And these signs will accompany those who believe: In my name they will drive out demons; they will speak in new tongues;"*

> *Acts 2:1-13 (NIV)*
> *"1 When the day of Pentecost came, they were all together in one place. 2 Suddenly a sound like the blowing of a violent wind came from heaven and filled the whole house where they were sitting. 3 They saw what seemed to be tongues of fire that separated and came to rest on each of them. 4 All of them were filled with the Holy Spirit and began to speak in other tongues as the Spirit enabled them. 5 Now there were staying in Jerusalem God-fearing Jews from every nation under heaven. 6 When they heard this sound, a crowd came together in bewilderment, because each one heard their own language*

being spoken. 7 Utterly amazed, they asked: "Aren't all these who are speaking Galileans? 8 Then how is it that each of us hears them in our native language? 9 Parthians, Medes and Elamites; residents of Mesopotamia, Judea and Cappadocia, Pontus and Asia, 10 Phrygia and Pamphylia, Egypt and the parts of Libya near Cyrene; visitors from Rome 11 (both Jews and converts to Judaism); Cretans and Arabs—we hear them declaring the wonders of God in our own tongues!" 12 Amazed and perplexed, they asked one another, "What does this mean?" 13 Some, however, made fun of them and said, "They have had too much wine.""

Peter stood up in their midst and remanded them that none of them were drunk from wine, but that it was the effect of the Holy Spirit's Baptism that caused them to behave and act in the way they did. It was the Holy Spirit's influence that enabled them to speak in languages, other than their own know language. It was the Gift of Tongues in full operation.

Acts 10:44-46 (NIV)
"44 While Peter was still speaking these words, the Holy Spirit came on all who heard the message. 45 The circumcised believers who had come with Peter were astonished that the gift of the Holy Spirit had been poured out even on Gentiles. 46 For they heard them speaking in tongues and praising God."

Acts 19:1-7 (NIV)
"1 While Apollos was at Corinth, Paul took the road through the interior and arrived at Ephesus. There he found some disciples 2 and asked them, "Did you receive the Holy Spirit when you believed?" They answered, "No, we have not even heard that there is a Holy Spirit." 3 So Paul asked, "Then what baptism did you receive?" "John's baptism," they replied. 4 Paul said, "John's baptism was a baptism of repentance. He told the people to believe in the one coming after him, that is, in Jesus." 5 On

hearing this, they were baptized in the name of the Lord Jesus. 6 When Paul placed his hands on them, the Holy Spirit came on them, and they spoke in tongues and prophesied. 7 There were about twelve men in all."

1 Corinthians 12:10,28 (NIV)
"10 to another miraculous powers, to another prophecy, to another distinguishing between spirits, to another speaking in different kinds of tongues, and to still another the interpretation of tongues. 28 And God has placed in the church first of all apostles, second prophets, third teachers, then miracles, then gifts of healing, of helping, of guidance, and of different kinds of tongues."

1 Corinthians 14:13-19 (NIV)
"13 For this reason the one who speaks in a tongue should pray that they may interpret what they say. 14 For if I pray in a tongue, my spirit prays, but my mind is unfruitful. 15 So what shall I do? I will pray with my spirit, but I will also pray with my understanding; I will sing with my spirit, but I will also sing with my understanding. 16 Otherwise when you are praising God in the Spirit, how can someone else, who is now put in the position of an inquirer, say "Amen" to your thanksgiving, since they do not know what you are saying? 17 You are giving thanks well enough, but no one else is edified. 18 I thank God that I speak in tongues more than all of you. 19 But in the church, I would rather speak five intelligible words to instruct others than ten thousand words in a tongue."

Discovery Questions.

The answers to the following few questions might be telltale signs that might help you to know whether you have received this gift.

- Have you received the gift of speaking in a language, you

have never learnt, but received this amazing ability when you received the Baptism in the Holy Spirit?
- Do you often sense, apart from your private prayer times, that God might bring a specific message to you and through you when you pray in the Spirit?
- Do you have a strong sense that God sometimes gives you a discernible message for His people while you speak in tongues?
- Have People told you that when you spoke in tongues, they felt how God spoke through you, and that the interpretation of the tongues confirmed it?
- Do you have a clear sense when you speak in tongues, whether it is a divine message, or merely yourself praying in the Spirit?

If the answer to all of these statements is a strong "**YES**" then you most certainly have been blessed by God in receiving this spiritual gift of speaking in tongues. If the answer is more "**YES, sometimes**" then you should certainly open yourself up to the possibility that the Lord desire to increasingly use you to bring divine message in tongues, that will ultimately bless and encourage others through it and its interpretation. If the answer is a "NO, I have never sensed such an urge or prompting, then you might be one of those precious believers who has been blessed with some other prominent gift to serve the Body of Christ.

9. Interpretation of Tongues

The Gift of Interpretation of Tongues is often experienced among Believers where someone, or the speaker self, receive a divinely inspired message in Tongues, and then understand a specific message through it to be delivered for the encouragement, exhortation or edification of the fellow Believers.

1 Corinthians 14:13 (NIV)
"13 For this reason the one who speaks in a tongue should pray that they may interpret what they say."

1 Corinthians 14:5 (NIV)
"5 I would like every one of you to speak in tongues, but I would rather have you prophesy. The one who prophesies is greater than the one who speaks in tongues, unless someone interprets, so that the church may be edified."

1 Corinthians 14:26-28 (NIV)
"26 What then shall we say, brothers and sisters? When you come together, each of you has a hymn, or a word of instruction, a revelation, a tongue or an interpretation. Everything must be done so that the church may be built up. 27 If anyone speaks in a tongue, two—or at the most three—should speak, one at a time, and someone must interpret. 28 If there is no interpreter, the speaker should keep quiet in the church and speak to himself and to God."

Discovery Questions.

The answers to the following few questions might be telltale signs that might help you to know whether you have received this gift.

- Do you often find yourself knowing what God wants to say to His people when someone brings a message in tongues?
- Do you often, instantaneously, receive the interpretation of tongues when someone bring a message in tongues?
- Do you find yourself knowing what people are saying even though you have no learnt knowledge of a language?
- Do you find yourself praying for the interpretation of tongues so that you might be used by God to bring messages of hope, through the interpretation, to build people up?

- Have you heard people say to you that the messages you brought in response to someone bring a message in tongues, spoke to them and encouraged them?

If the answer to all of these statements is a strong "YES" then you most certainly have been blessed by God in receiving this spiritual gift to teach others. If the answer is more "YES, sometimes" then you should certainly open yourself up to the possibility that the Lord desire to increasingly use you to teach others through you. If the answer is a "NO, I have never sensed such an urge or prompting," then you might be one of those precious believers who has been blessed with some other prominent gift to serve the Body of Christ.

Afterword

This concludes our brief journey to understanding the Supernatural Spiritual Gifts. During the concluding sessions of this encounter, we will complete a questionnaire to learn and know our Spiritual Gifts. We will also take this time to affirm the spiritual gifts in the lives of those who are here with us. I pray that the concluding parts of this weekend encounter will serve as great encouragement to you.

5

DISCOVERING YOUR SPIRITUAL GIFTS
SESSION FIVE

This guide has been developed to assist you in discovering your spiritual gifts, and it should not be viewed as a test. The only right answers here are honest and sincere answers. The answers you provide will help you find the areas where the Holy Spirit' enablement might be best applied to building the church up.

Before You Start

Follow These Six Steps:

Step 1 - Print out the answer sheet from the following pages.

Go through the list of 100 statements on the questionnaire. For each one, mark on the answer sheet to what extent the statement is true of your life:
    3 = **MOSTLY,** or
    2 = **SOMETIMES,** or
    1 = **LITTLE,** or
    0 = **NOT AT ALL**

Discovering Your Spiritual Gifts | 83

Be Careful! Do not score according to what you think should be true or hope might be true in the future. Be honest and score on the basis of present and recent experiences. If you are a young Christian or new in the faith, the results will need extra care in interpretation.

Step 2 - Score your questionnaire.

When you are finished, score the questionnaire according to the instructions on the scoring sheet.

Step 3 – Identify your top 3 Gifts.

Identify the top 3 to 5 gifts where you scored 10 or more.

Step 4 – Affirm each others top 3 Gifts.

Ask a close friend within the group, or even your Pastor, to score you by identifying your top 3 gifts as they see them. See whether this confirms your scoring. In most cases, unless the person assessing you does not know you at all, the assessor will probably affirm 80 to 100% the most prominent gifts of God on your life.

Step 5 - Study your gifts.

Specifically Study the gift definitions and Scripture references of those gifts where you had a 10 or above score. Look for ways in which you can develop them more, or where you can open yourself up to be used by the Holy Spirit to use you more within those identified areas.

Step 6 – Use your gifts.

Use these gifts in your ministry to build the Body of Christ up, and always be on the quest to eagerly desire more spiritual gifts to use.

VORSTER SPIRITUAL GIFTS QUESTIONAIRE.

For each statement, mark to what extent it is true in your life:
- 3 = MOSTLY, or
- 2 = SOMETIMES, or
- 1 = LITTLE, or
- 0 = NOT AT ALL

Now, turn over to the **VORSTER SPIRITUAL GIFTS DISCOVERY QUESTION SHEET**

6

VORSTER SPIRITUAL GIFTS QUESTIONNAIRE

SESSION SIX

For each of the 100 statements, mark to what extent it is true in your life:

Place the appropriate number, as it is most true in your life, next to each statement.

3 = MOSTLY, or
2 = SOMETIMES, or
1 = LITTLE, or
0 = NOT AT ALL

Mark the 100 statements in the Vorster Questionnaire in the following few pages!

VORSTER SPIRITUAL GIFTS DISCOVERY QUESTION SHEET			
No.	Gifts discovery questions	Score
1	I often receive and deliver direct messages from God that edify, exhort or comfort others.	
2	I enjoy helping to do ordinary tasks that will make things easier for others.	
3	I have heard that I have helped Believers learn truths from the Bible through my sharing.	
4	I quite naturally and spontaneous see the positive side of sometimes difficult situations.	
5	I am quite disciplined in managing my finances well, as to enable me to give generously to the Lord's work.	
6	I find it easy to make decisions that others are willing to follow.	
7	I have a strong preference to help those who are physically and mentally challenged, and to help alleviate their suffering.	
8	I find it easy to apply biblical principles, in context, in my own life.	
9	I often find that the Holy Spirit gives me insight about people I have no prior knowledge about.	

Vorster Spiritual Gifts Questionnaire Q 1-9

10	I find it fairly easy to take on new assignments I sense the Lord instructs me to do.	
11	I have been used by God to pray for the sick and they received their healing.	
12	I often see extra-ordinary miracles take place when I pray in the Name of the Lord Jesus.	
13	I often find myself being able to see through the pretenses of people, even before it was evident to other people.	
14	I have received the gift of speaking in a language I have never learnt but received this amazing ability when I received the Holy Spirit.	
15	I often find myself being able to instantly know what the Lord wants to say to His people when someone brings a message in tongues.	
16	I feel like God anointed me as a leader, especially when I am with other Believers.	
17	I feel like God anointed me as someone who sees things, before they happen.	
18	I have been able to lead people to accept Jesus as their Lord and Saviour.	
19	I feel like God anointed me as someone to take care of other Believers.	
20	I feel like God anointed me to teach other Believers the deep things of God.	

Vorster Spiritual Gifts Questionnaire Q 10-20

21	I have received from the Holy Spirit and proclaimed specific things that will happen in the future, and it happened just as I saw it.
22	I always find joy in cleaning, setting things up, or packing things up after ministry opportunities.
23	I love seeing people gain new insights in God's Word from my sharing with them.
24	I always find some uplifting and positive thing to say to others.
25	I give considerably more than a tithe of my income to the Lord's work, and this is reflected in my monthly budget records.
26	I find that people generally look to me for guidance in what needs to be done.
27	I have cared for others when they have had material or physical needs.
28	I often find myself coming up with solutions to fairly complicated situations.
29	I often receive and share insights of spiritual situations with people that help bring them closer to God.
30	I often do things that's not been done or attempted before, purely because I sense the leading of the Holy Spirit in doing it.
31	I often see spiritually troubled people healed through my prayers and ministry.
32	I often see demon spirits come out of people when I minister to them.

Vorster Spiritual Gifts Questionnaire Q 21-32

33	I often see the specific Call and Purpose of God on certain people.
34	I often sense, apart from my private prayer times, that God might bring a specific message through me when I pray in the Spirit.
35	I often pray and receive the interpretation when someone speaks in tongues.
36	I have an assurance that wherever God might call me to a new place, or assignment, that I will be able to lead people to Christ and care for them.
37	I have delivered messages, at the right time, that impacted people's lives greatly.
38	I often share my testimony to others of how the Lord saved me, and then see them put their faith in Jesus Christ as well.
39	I love taking care of the spiritual needs and welfare of Believers.
40	I love teaching Believers the word of God in a systematic and logically understandable way.
41	I have been told that specific personal messages I brought to people, under the inspiration of the Holy Spirit, must have come from the Lord, since it happened just as the Lord said
42	I always look for opportunities to help with menial tasks to make things easier for others.

43	I love to study God's Word and look for things not seen or understood before.	
44	I daily take time to compliment others.	
45	I am often asked to give to some Kingdom Advancing causes, and by the Grace of God I am able to find the funds to give towards such causes.	
46	I am often asked to give directives in what needs to happen next.	
47	I am often asked to visit people in hospitals and in troublesome circumstances.	
48	I frequently find myself guiding Believers to finding solutions from Biblical examples and stories.	
49	I often find divine strategies and techniques, through my time in the Bible and prayer, that God seem to use in furthering His kingdom.	
50	I frequently find myself stepping out in faith to do things.	
51	I frequently find myself in ministry situations where I pray for unwell people and where they receive instant healing.	
52	I frequently find myself in ministry situations where I pray for the impossible to become possible and then it happens just as I prayed.	
53	I have a strong sense of assurance to discern when a person is afflicted by an evil spirit.	

Vorster Spiritual Gifts Questionnaire Q 43-53

54	I have a strong sense that God sometimes gives me a discernable message for His people while I speak in tongues.	
55	I have a strong sense to discern what people say even though I do not know the language.	
56	I often see that people do what I ask them to do without questioning me.	
57	I have deeply upset people when I brought them the Message God gave me to give to them.	
58	I often see how people respond positively to the gospel message when I deliver it.	
59	I feel much more comfortable to work with people with whom I developed a relationship over a long period of time, and to share in their daily wellbeing.	
60	I feel comfortable to defend the truths of God's Word against false beliefs.	
61	I often have a strong sense of what God wants to say to people in relation to their particular situations.	
62	I prefer to do the hard work behind the scenes to help the work of God go smoothly.	
63	I often take time to think about ways in which to share the truths of God's Word more effectively to help Believers in their walk with God.	

Vorster Spiritual Gifts Questionnaire Q 54-63

64	I often hear that my positive attitude and words encourage people.
65	I often give sacrificially and commit to give consistently, even though it stretches me at times beyond what I have in hand, just because of my faith in a matter, and because of my love to sow into God's work.
66	My ideas and suggestions are usually accepted by most as the way to move forward.
67	I love to give my time to help people find solutions and outcomes to their problems.
68	I often hear that the biblical truth I share is most relevant and specific to the felt needs of fellow believers.
69	I daily seek to understand what God desires to say to His People, that lines up with the Bible
70	I often hear that people admire me for the bold steps I take to advance the work of God.
71	I often hear that people bring honour to God for healing them through my prayers and ministry.
72	I often find myself in situations where supernatural provisions and breakthroughs occur after my prayers and declarations.
73	I quickly recognize whether a person is teaching something he received from God, from Satan, or of himself.

Vorster Spiritual Gifts Questionnaire Q 64-73

74	People have told me that when I spoke in tongues, they felt how God spoke through me, and that the interpretation of the tongues confirmed it.	
75	I always pray that God will give me understanding when people speak in tongues that I might encourage and bring messages of hope that will build people up.	
76	I always have a burning desire to be sent out to start a new church.	
77	I always have a burning desire to hear from God and bring messages of hope and encouragement to His People.	
78	It gives me great satisfaction to tell people how to put their faith in Jesus Christ to be their Lord and Saviour.	
79	I have this notion to want to build deep and meaningful relationships with people, and through that interaction, to serve them better.	
80	I know the doctrines of the Bible and love sharing them with Believers.	
81	I often feel that I know exactly what God wants to say and do in a meeting and what specific ministry is needed at a specific point in time.	
82	I feel privileged to be able to serve others by doing the unthankful tasks.	

Vorster Spiritual Gifts Questionnaire Q 74-82

83	I feel honored to see people grow in their faith as a result of my sharing the truths of God's Word with them.	
84	I feel privileged to have a naturally positive outlook and that I am able to show people the good and blessed things in their lives.	
85	I have consistently lowered my standard of living in order to advance God's work.	
86	I find it easy to make thought-through decisions.	
87	I feel blessed and called to help those in less fortunate physical, mental or material circumstances.	
88	I often sense great peace and personal confidence when important decisions need to be made.	
89	I often find that the Holy Spirit gives me knowledge and insight about situations firsthand.	
90	I often do things when I have a sense of great personal conviction.	
91	I often have a sense to pray for the sick in my ministry, and then see amazing healings take place.	
92	I often pray for the blind, deaf and cripple, and then see amazing miracles take place.	
93	I can usually tell immediately whether a person speaking in tongues is bringing a divine message, or merely praying in the Spirit, or faking it.	

Vorster Spiritual Gifts Questionnaire Q 83-93

94	I have a clear sense when I speak in tongues, whether it is a divine message, or me merely praying in the Spirit.	
95	I have heard others say to me that the words I spoke after someone spoke in tongues really spoke to them and built them up and encourage them.	
96	I often get asked to serve in leadership positions because of my ability to make things happen.	
97	I often get asked to pray about situations and hear what God says to do in those situations.	
98	I often hear people say that it was through my sharing the gospel message, that they were saved.	
99	I often hear people say that I am a good friend, especially since I am always there for them, understand them, and care for them.	
100	I often hear people say that I am a good Teacher of the Word of God.	

Vorster Spiritual Gifts Questionnaire Q 94-100

In Conclusion

In the next session we will add the results to determine the specific gifts God gave you already.

7

VORSTER GIFTS SCORE SHEET
SESSION SEVEN

In this session we will tally up the scores we gave each of the questions in the Vorster Spiritual Gifts Discovery Questionnaire.

Instructions for Scoring

1. Turn to your Score Sheet, towards the back of the book, after reading these instructions.
2. Add your Score Sheet answers together, from left to right, and write that total in the Totals box next to each gift.

Example: Add together the number you wrote in box 1, plus the number in box 21, plus the number in box 41, plus the number in box 61 and the number in box 81. Those five numbers, added together, become your total score to be written in the **TOTAL** box.

VORSTER GIFTS SCORE SHEET						
Write down scores from questionnaire here.					Total score	Rank results	GIFTS
1	21	41	61	81			Prophecy
2	22	42	62	82			Serving
3	23	43	63	83			Teaching
4	24	44	64	84			Exhortation
5	25	45	65	85			Giving
6	26	46	66	86			Leading
7	27	47	67	87			Mercy
8	28	48	68	88			Words of Wisdom
9	29	49	69	89			Words of Knowledge
10	30	50	70	90			Faith
11	31	51	71	91			Gifts of Healing
12	32	52	72	92			Working of Miracles
13	33	53	73	93			Discerning of Spirits
14	34	54	74	94			Tongues
15	35	55	75	95			Interpretation of Tongues
16	36	56	76	96			Apostle
17	37	57	77	97			Prophet
18	38	58	78	98			Evangelist
19	39	59	79	99			Pastor
20	40	60	80	100			Teacher

Vorster Gifts Score Sheet

Directions

When you have finished responding to all 100 statements and scored your test, follow the instructions listed below for better understanding.

STEP 1

After adding up your points, you should have several notably high scores. These are your probable spiritual gifts. Please indicate them below, starting with your highest score. Any score below 9, however, is probably not a positive indicator of a gift. If you had other high scores, or if you feel sure you have certain gifts even though they didn't receive high marks, put them down as well. You have just taken the first step toward discovering your spiritual gifts. Please understand that this exercise only indicates your probable gifts. Over the next few weeks you should use the following five steps to more clearly determine your spiritual gifts.

STEP 2

Pray, believing that God will continue to reveal to you what gifts He has given you. Don't forget 1 Cor. 12:11: Gifts have been distributed "to each individual." Pray also for the wisdom and desire to use your gifts with the greatest efficiency for Him.

STEP 3

Study the Bible passages that deal specifically with this topic: Romans 12, 1 Corinthians 12-14, Ephesians 3, 4 and 1 Peter 4. And take time to reflect on the contexts of the many Bible stories of men and women who used their gifts for God. Such accounts serve as examples and as inspiration.

STEP 4

Experiment by using your new-found gifts. This may be a new experience, and you may not know where to start. See the next page for some suggestions. As you begin to work for God, your gifts will develop in an exciting way.

STEP 5

Confirm the gifts of others. When you see another person using his gift effectively, say so. This isn't flattery, it's a vital step in the ongoing process of spiritual gift development.

Let's begin this process right away. Please mark down the spiritual gifts you've observed in three fellow Christians in your congregation. Your keen observations will be appreciated by each of them and your pastor.

This is a good opportunity to let your friends know what their gifts are, simply by listing them here. It's also a good time to let them know, in a very gracious (and anonymous) way, what their gifts aren't by leaving those gifts off the list. Make this an honest appraisal.

The summary of gifts beginning on the next page may help you in your evaluation.

STEP 6

Expect confirmation of your gifts by other church members. Following your handing in this inventory to your pastor, your inventory will be returned with a listing of some of the gifts your fellow believers have observed in you. Everyone who hands in his inventory should receive an evaluation. You may not agree with this evaluation! But instead of dismissing these opinions, explore them. Look for ways to develop the abilities others believe you possess.

. . .

Take a moment now to write down the scores from questionnaire here.

Write down the Top three Gifts according to your score results.
YOUR SPIRITUAL GIFTS
1.
2.
3.

Do the result surprise you? _____
What did you think they were before you started?
1.
2.
3.

Take a moment to score at least two friends.
FRIENDS SPIRITUAL GIFTS
FRIEND:_____
1.
2.
3.
FRIEND:_____
1.
2.
3.

Ask your Pastor or Spiritual Leader for their assessment:
PASTOR'S SPIRITUAL GIFT ASSESSMENT OF YOU:
1.
2.
3.

Spiritual Gifts List:

Prophecy
    Serving
    Teaching
    Exhortation
    Giving
    Leading
    Mercy
    Words of Wisdom
    Words of Knowledge
    Faith
    Gifts of Healing
    Working of Miracles
    Discerning of Spirits
    Tongues
    Interpretation of Tongues
    Apostle
    Prophet
    Evangelist
    Pastor
    Teacher

IN CLOSING

I pray that you too found this very inspirational, as many thousands of other Believers had in the past. I pray that you will pursue Spiritual Gifts that will build and encourage the Body of Christ, especially the Gift of Prophecy.

> *1 Peter 4:10 (NIV)* **"Each of you should use whatever gift you have received to serve others,** *as faithful stewards of God's grace in its various forms.* **If anyone speaks,** *they should do so as one who speaks the very words of God.* **If anyone serves,** *they*

should do so with the strength God provides, so that in all things God may be praised through Jesus Christ. To him be the glory and the power for ever and ever. Amen."

Use the Gifts God gave you to build the Church up. May Jesus be glorified through the way you use the Gifts of the Holy Spirit.

PART II

OTHER BOOKS BY DR. HENDRIK J VORSTER

OTHER BOOKS BY DR HENDRIK J VORSTER

Discipleship Foundations - Step One - Salvation Disciple Manual

Step One - Salvation

This Course explores the "How to" be Born Again and to establish a solid Foundation for your faith in Jesus Christ. It is based on Hebrews chapter 6 verses 1 and 2, and explores:
    Repentance of dead works,
    Faith in God,
    Baptisms,
    Laying on of hands,
    Resurrection of the dead, and
    Eternal Judgement

Teacher Manuals and Video Teaching material are available from our website: www.churchplantinginstitute.com

Step Two - Values and Spiritual Disciplines Disciple Manual

Discipleship Foundations Step Two - Values and Spiritual Disciplines Disciple Manual

This Course explores the "How to" develop spiritual disciplines as well as 52 Values Jesus taught. It is based on the teachings of Jesus to His Disciples, and explores:

Spiritual Disciplines

The disciplines we explore are: Reading, meditating on the Word of God, Prayer, Stewardship, Fasting, Servanthood, Simplicity, Worship, and Witnessing.

Values of the Kingdom of God

Humility, Mournfulness, meekness, Spiritual Passion, Mercifulness, Purity, Peacemaker, Patient endurance, Example, Custodian, Reconciliatory, Resoluteness, Loving, Discreetness, Forgiving, Kingdom of God Investor, God-minded, Kingdom of God prioritiser, Introspective, Persistent, Considerate, Conservative, Fruit-bearing, Practitioner, Accountability, Faithful, Childlikeness, Unity, Servanthood, Loyalty, Gratefulness, Stewardship, Obedience, Carefulness, Compassion, Caring, Confidence, Steadfastness, Contentment, Teachable, Deference, Diligence, Trustworthiness, Gentleness, Discernment, Truthfulness, Generous, Kindness, Watchfulness, Perseverance, Honouring and Submissive.

Teacher Manuals and Video Teaching material are available from our website: www.churchplantinginstitute.com

Discipleship Foundations Step Three - Developing Gifts and Skills

Step Three - Developing Gifts and Skills

This course is run through five weekend encounters. These weekend encounters have been designed to help Disciples discover their spiritual gifts, as well as learn skills to use their gifts, and to serve the Lord for the extension of His Kingdom. The Weekend Encounters are:

Gifts Discovery Weekend Encounter

We learn about Ministerial Office gifts, Service gifts, and Supernatural Spiritual Gifts. We discover our own, and then learn How we may use them to build up the local Church.

Survey of the Bible Weekend Encounter

During this weekend we do a survey of the Bible, from Genesis to Revelation. We also learn about the History of the Bible as well as How we can make most of our time in the Word.

Sharing your Faith Weekend Encounter

During this weekend we learn about the Gospel message, and How to share our faith effectively.

Overcoming Weekend Encounter

During this weekend we deal with those thistles and thorns that smother the growth and harvest of the good seed sown into our lives. We address How to overcome fear, unforgiveness, lust and the cares of the world with faith and obedience.

Shepherd Leader Weekend Encounter

During this weekend encounter we learn about being a Good Shepherd, and How to best disciple in a small group.

Teacher Manuals and Video Teaching material are available from our website: www.churchplantinginstitute.com

Discipleship Foundations Step Four - Fruitfulness

Step Four - Fruitfulness

We were saved to serve. This course has been designed to mobilise Believers from Learners to Practitioners. These sessions have been prepared for individual use with those who are producing fruit.

We explore:

1. Introduction.
2. Walking with purpose.
3. Build purposeful relationships. Finding Worthy Men
4. Priesthood. Praying effectively for those entrusted to you.
5. Caring compassionately.
6. Walking worthily.
7. Walking in the Spirit.
8. Practicing hospitality.

Teacher Manuals and Video Teaching material are available from our website: www.churchplantinginstitute.com

Step Five - Multiplication

Discipleship Foundations Step Five - Multiplication

This course was designed to assist fruit-producing disciples to live a life that will encourage a lifetime of fruitfulness. It will also give disciples skills and guidelines to navigate their disciples through seasons of challenge and growth. We explore:

1. Vision and dreams.
2. Set Godly Goals.
3. Character development
4. Gifts development
Impartation and Activation
5. Fruitfulness comes through constant challenge.
6. Relationships
Family, Children and Friends
7. The Power of encouragement
8. Finances
Personal and Ministry finances
9. Dealing with setbacks

- How to deal with failure?
- How to deal with betrayal?
- How to deal with rejection?
- How to deal with trials?
- How to deal with despondency?

10. Eternal rewards

Teacher Manuals and Video Teaching material are available from our website: www.churchplantinginstitute.com

VALUES
OF THE
KINGDOM
OF
GOD

Dr. Hendrik J. Vorster

Values of the Kingdom of God
By Dr. Hendrik J Vorster

Everyone desires to be known as a pleasant to be around with kind of person. This book helps you develop values towards such a godly character. This book explores 52 Values of the Kingdom of God.

Books are available from our website: www.churchplantinginstitute.com

SPIRITUAL
DISCIPLINES
OF THE
KINGDOM
OF
GOD

Spiritual Disciplines of the Kingdom of God
By Dr. Hendrik J Vorster

Every Believer desires to be a Fruit-producing branch in the Vineyard of our Lord. Developing spiritual disciplines is to develop spiritual roots from which our faith can draw sap to grow strong and fruit-bearing branches. This Book explores Nine Spiritual Disciplines of the Kingdom of God.

Books are available from our website: www.churchplantinginstitute.com

Other Books by Dr Hendrik J Vorster

Church Planting - by Dr Hendrik J Vorster

Church Planting - How to plant a dynamic, disciple-making church
By Dr Hendrik J Vorster

This is a handbook for those who wish to plant a disciple-making church. This book explores every aspect of church planting, and is widely used in over 70 Nations on 6 Continents. Here is a list of the areas that are explored:

1. The challenge to plant New Churches
2. Phases of Church Planting
3. Phase One of Church Planting - The Calling, Vision and Preparation Phase
4. The Call to Church Planting
5. Twelve Characteristics of Church Planting Leaders
6. Church Planting Terminology
7. Phase Two of Church Planting - Discipleship
8. The Process of Discipleship
9. Phase Three of Church Planting - Congregating the Discipleship Groups
10. Understanding Church Planting Finances
11. Understanding Church staff
12. Phase Four of Church Planting - Ministry development and Church Launching Phase
13. Understanding and Implementing Systems
14. Phase Five of Church Planting - Multiplication
15. Understanding the challenges in Church Planting
16. How to succeed in Church Planting
17. How to plant a House Church

Student Manuals and Video Teaching material are available from our website: www.churchplantinginstitute.com

Discipleship Foundation Series on Video

Dr. Vorster teaching via Video

185 Video Teachings are available for each of the Sessions taught throughout these Discipleship Courses.

Discipleship Foundation Series

We have Five, completely recorded, Discipleship Courses available on Video at www.discipleshipcourses.com

- **Step One - Salvation** (*This 7-week course helps the new Believer to establish, and build a solid Foundation for their faith to build on.*) This course is available, **without charge**, upon free registration.
- **Step Two - Values and Spiritual Disciplines** (*This 9-week Course helps the young Believer to put down Spiritual Roots, by establishing spiritual disciplines, and by learning the values of the Kingdom of God.*)
- **Step Three - Developing Gifts and Skills** (*This Course is usually presented during 5 Weekend Encounters, or over a 23-week period. We explore Spiritual Gifts and How to use them*

to build up the local Church. We **explore the Bible**, and its origins, during one part to ensure we build our lives on the Handbook of the Bible. We also learn **How to share our faith.** We learn **How to deal with Strongholds** that might hold us back in fulfilling God's purpose. And finally, we learn **How to best Mentor** those whom we lead to Christ.)

- **Step Four - Discipling Fruit-Producers** (*During this 8-week course* we learn How to teach our Disciples the principles that will develop, and maintain, fruitfulness.)
- **Step Five - Multiplication** (*During this 11-week Course* we learn **How to Mentor our Leaders** to lead strong and healthy Fruit-producers.)

Free registration for access to these Video resources is available at www.dicipleshipcourses.com

Church Planting Training Videos

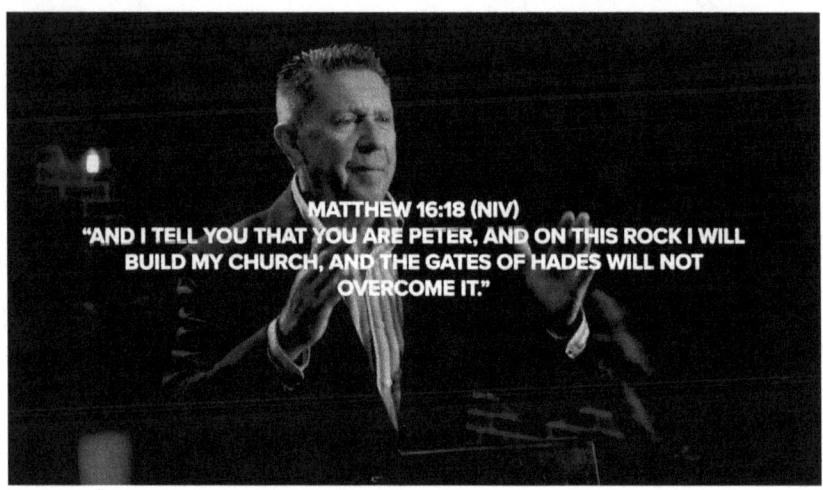

Dr. Vorster teaching via Video

42 Video Teachings are available in this **Church Planting Course.**

- Introduction to Church Planting
- Why plant New Churches?
- Phases of Church Planting Overview
- Phase 1 - Preparation Phase
- Phase 2 - Team Building Phase
- Phase 3 - Prelaunch Phase
- Phase 4 - Launch Phase
- Phase 5 - Multiplication Phase
- Church Planting Trials
- Next Steps

Free Enrolment is available at www.churchplantingcourses.com

Advanced Coaching sessions are available for those who enrolled in the Masters Training Program.

ENDNOTES

3. The Service Gifts

1. https://biblehub.com/greek/4394.htm
2. https://www.biblestudytools.com/lexicons/greek/nas/didasko.html